W9-CUZ-558

Perspectives on
Scripture
and
Tradition

Edited by Joseph F. Kelly

Perspectives on
Scripture and Tradition

Essays by
Robert M. Grant
Robert E. McNally,
George H. Tavard

Fides Publishers, Inc.
Notre Dame, Indiana

© COPYRIGHT 1976:   FIDES PUBLISHERS, INC.
NOTRE DAME, INDIANA 46556

Library of Congress Cataloging in Publication Data

Grant, Robert McQueen, 1917–
    Perspectives on Scripture and tradition.

    (The Walter and Mary Tuohy Chair lectures; 1974–
1975)
    Includes bibliographical references.
    CONTENTS: Grant, R. M. The creation of the Christian
tradition. From tradition to Scripture and back.—
McNally, R. E. Christian tradition and the early Middle
Ages. Tradition at the beginning of the Reformation.—
Tavard, G. H. Tradition in theology: A problematic
approach. A methodological approach.
    1. Bible and tradition—Addresses, essays, lectures.
I. McNally, Robert E. II. Tavard, Georges Henri,
1922– III. Title. IV. Series.
BT89.G68   220.6   76-2497
ISBN 0-8190-0617-3

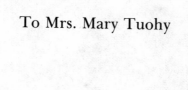

To Mrs. Mary Tuohy

CONTENTS

CONTENTS

Foreword

In 1966, Mrs. Mary Tuohy established the Walter and Mary Tuohy Chair of Interreligious Studies at John Carroll University in memory of her husband, Walter Tuohy, a prominent Cleveland industrialist. The purpose of the chair, unique in the United States, is to bring to the university outstanding scholars to offer classes and public lectures on topics of ecumenical and interreligious interest. In the 1974–1975 academic year, the topic of the Tuohy Chair was Scripture and Tradition; the recipients of the chair were Robert M. Grant, Robert E. McNally, S.J., and George H. Tavard.

The topic is an important ecumenical issue for Christians. In recent years various denominations have established harmonious working relationships with one another and have found common ground on many issues. But agreement is not unity. Christians who believe in the same God differ from one another in their credal statements and often by the theological formulations of those statements. When Christians can accept similar credal statements, unity will be advanced.

But common statements presume a common authority, and here the problem lies. Since the reformations of the sixteenth century, the various denominations have emphasized different sources of theological and doctrinal authority. The classical Protestant statement, *scriptura sola,* denied the authority of extrabiblical sources. The response of the Counter-Reformation was to exalt extrabiblical sources, under the heading of tradition, a process culminating in the definition of papal infallibility at the First Vatican Council in 1870.

But the dichotomy of Protestant-scripture and Catholic-tradition is too simplistic. Roman Catholic theological methodology, formulated by the sixteenth-century scholastic Melchior Cano, always began with scripture, and even Martin Luther, champion of "scripture alone," found it necessary to write volumes of commentaries to explain God's word to the people. From the sixteenth century to today, the relation of scripture and tradition has been one of the most significant and complex problems in Christian thought. Indeed, before it became an ecumenical issue, scripture and tradition provided the background and framework for many theological and doctrinal questions.

The program of the 1974–1975 Tuohy Chair examined this problem from three perspectives: scriptural, historical and contemporary. The program was in two parts. First, there was a series of classes for university undergraduates. In these classes, Mr. Grant discussed the New Testament and patristic aspects of the question, Father McNally the Medieval and Reformation aspects, and Father Tavard the contemporary attitudes toward scripture and tradition. Thus the students were able to obtain a brief but authoritative overview of the question.

The second part of the program consisted of six public lectures, two by each of the chair recipients. These lectures, here published, were not intended as an inclusive portrayal of scripture and tradition, but rather as perspectives of foremost scholars on particular aspects of the question. As such, they have great value for those interested in ecumenism, theological methodology, and, of course, scripture and tradition.

The lectures were given at John Carroll University during the period of 6 January to 14 January 1975 to an appreciative audience of students, guests and the general public. The university is happy to make these lectures available to a wider audience.

John Carroll University   JOSEPH F. KELLY
Cleveland, Ohio

The Contributors

ROBERT M. GRANT is Carl Darling Buck Professor of Humanities at the University of Chicago. He is a foremost authority on the New Testament and the patristic period. He has published many books and articles, including *Gnosticism and Early Christianity* and *Augustus to Constantine*.

ROBERT E. McNALLY, S.J., is Professor of Historical Theology at Fordham University. He is a leading historian of exegesis in the Medieval and Reformation periods. His many publications include *The Bible in the Early Middle Ages* and *The Unreformed Church*.

GEORGE H. TAVARD is Professor of Theology at the Methodist Theological School in Ohio. A *peritus* at Vatican II, he is an expert on the theology of tradition. His writings in this area include *Holy Writ or Holy Church?* and *La Tradition au XVIIe Siècle*.

The Editor

JOSEPH F. KELLY is Assistant Professor of Historical Theology at John Carroll University. He has published a book and some articles on the history of exegesis.

CHAPTER ONE

The Creation of the Christian Tradition

Robert M. Grant

When the Persian religious leader Mani, founder of the religion named after him, was writing books to show that his revelation was superior to what Buddha, Zoroaster, and Jesus had taught, he argued that one error of his predecessors had been to rely on personal example and influence without writing things down themselves. Naturally the teaching of Jesus and the others had been distorted when they were no longer with their disciples. Mani's own religion would last till the end of the world because he wrote books.[1]

This was not an absolutely new approach to the Christian tradition, even in the third century, when Mani taught. In fact, something rather like it had already been expressed in the second century by the great Christian heretic Marcion. Marcion admired the insights expressed by Paul in the major epistles and did not like the Jewish Jesus presented in the synoptic gospels. One reason for his lack of enthusiasm was that in his time the Romans had just crushed a violent Jewish revolt in Palestine; he was not eager to be associated with the rebels. Whatever the cause of his attitude, Marcion believed that only Paul had been able to understand Jesus, and Paul did so by means of a revelation, not a tradition (Gal. 1:12). In Marcion's view what had happened was that Jesus taught a pure gospel like the one Paul knew, but his

1

Jewish disciples, eager to preach the gospel to Jews, drastically revised it to meet the religious needs of their hearers. Only Marcion himself, relying on the true, consistent gospel expressed by Paul, was able to revise the one fairly reliable gospel written by Luke and remove the interpolations from it. Thus, Marcion could get back to the single, correct written gospel as it should have existed from the beginning of Christianity.[2]

Actually, of course, the situation was not that neat or clear. Both Mani and Marcion wanted religions more exactly definable than Christianity was. For in the Christian situation we begin with gospel, go on to tradition, move into scripture, renew tradition. There is a never-ending process, one which might almost be called dialectical. There is a tension between tradition and scripture, never an absolute separation of one from the other, never—in the early church—a situation in which one had to choose between scripture or tradition, at least within the church. Most members of the church would reject both the scriptures and the traditions of the Gnostics. The conflict was not over scripture-or-tradition.

In the New Testament, tradition is presented in two ways, diametrically opposed to each other. Or it would be better to say that two kinds of traditions are so presented. The first is the kind of legal tradition for interpreting the Old Testament which Jesus rejected. Both Mark and Matthew devote sections in their gospels to this rejection. There are traditions, chiefly having to do with popular religious practices, that have grown up alongside the Old Testament law. Jesus rejects them as merely "the tradition of the elders" or "the tradition of men" (Mark 7; Matt. 15). What counts is "the commandment of God," as given, for example, by Moses in the decalogue. Even in a late epistle we find the idea that popular religious practices, perhaps related to theosophy, are "in accordance with the tradition of men."

They are merely human, not divinely authorized. This is one way, the negative way, of looking at tradition. It is the way taken by reformers who no longer find particular traditions acceptable. The traditions basically in question here are the traditions developed in Judaism, chiefly by Pharisees in order to make the Old Testament law workable. We might compare the content of these traditions with the science of casuistry.

The other kind of tradition encountered in the New Testament is found especially in the apostle Paul's letter to the Corinthians. These are Christian traditions. Paul praises at least some of his readers on the ground that they are maintaining the traditions that he delivered to them (1 Cor. 11:2; a similar idea in 2 Thess. 2:15). What are such traditions? A brief look through First Corinthians will show us. First, in the seventh chapter Paul has to deal with the troublesome question of divorce and remarriage. In his whole discussion he keeps coming back to the question of what, according to the tradition, Jesus the Lord had said on the subject. "To those who are married I give orders—not I but the Lord—that a woman is not to be separated from her husband (if she is separated, she is to remain unmarried or be reconciled to her husband), and a man is not to leave his wife" (7:10–11). This statement about the Lord's original command is especially significant because it is like one form of the gospel tradition, unlike another. It is like Mark 10:11–12, which speaks of a man's divorcing his wife and a wife's divorcing her husband. But the saying of Jesus in this form has already undergone interpretation within the church. In Palestinian Judaism, in the circumstances in which he made his original pronouncement, a woman could not divorce her husband anyway. It seems highly likely, therefore, that what Jesus actually said has been better reflected in Matthew 15:9, which speaks only of the man's divorcing the woman. Paul probably did not know that the saying had been generalized. On the other hand, it might not have made much difference to him had he known it. He might well have assumed that what the tradition was and what the tradition implied did not need to be separated. What did need to be separated? What did need to be separated, in his view, was what he had added entirely on his own. "To the others," he wrote (by others he means "Christians married to pagans"), "I say, not the Lord." The reason for this is obvious. During the ministry of Jesus there was no occasion for any statements about the mixed marriages typical of a fairly settled community. Paul supplies his own rules, and explicitly says he is doing so; he can differentiate his own teaching from that of the Lord, at least sometimes. Finally he adds that on unmarried persons he has no command of the Lord; he simply gives counsel as one whom the Lord allowed to be a reliable witness (7:25). On widows, too, he has advice to give. "I suppose that I too have the spirit of God," he concludes (7:40).

What this chapter gives us is a fascinating blend of authoritative tradition, derived from the Lord and transmitted, with interpretation, through the Christian communities, with the Apostle's own decisions on matters related to the tradition, authoritative because of his apostolic call (7:25) and his possession of the spirit of God (7:40). This is to say that in his view the original tradition is not something absolutely fixed or static. It is a tradition which could have been, was, and is being supplemented and reinterpreted as it was and is handed down.

The second passage in First Corinthians which we should notice is one in which Paul is arguing that Christian missionaries have the right to be supported by their converts (9:3–14). The passage is rather strange, since Paul uses so many different kinds of arguments to prove his point. The other apostles even (it seems) have their wives' expenses paid; why should not Barnabas and Paul receive funds?

Soldiers and shepherds are paid the equivalent of wages. A text in Deuteronomy speaks of not muzzling an ox on the threshing-floor; this must refer to people, not oxen, and indeed to missionaries. Priests and Levites get paid. And now, finally, after all these examples, Paul says that "so also the Lord commanded that those who proclaim the gospel should live off the gospel." If any of the sayings in our canonical gospels is in view, presumably it is Luke 10:7, "the workman deserves his wage," or Matthew 10:10, with a reference to food. In the context of either gospel, the sayings mean what Paul says his tradition means. But it is very odd that he refrains from using the authority of the Lord up to the very last minute. Perhaps he was aware that much of his argument was not especially convincing. (Echoes of it, in much simpler form, seem to recur in Galatians 6:6 and Romans 15:27.) Conceivably this can be explained by assuming that Paul was actually the first Christian writer, or thought he was the first Christian writer, to discuss this topic, and the saying of the Lord came to his attention or out of his memory only after his argument was well under way. It is this saying, from oral tradition, however, which ends his series of proofs. It is the clincher.

We already have referred to Paul's mention of traditions in 1 Corinthians 11:2. Now we should observe that such a mention occurs at the beginning of another collection of rather feeble arguments. This time the tradition in question has nothing to do with any saying of the Lord. Paul simply wants to argue that women should wear veils in church, and he has no really adequate grounds for his case. Actually the case is far from strong. Corinthian women did not wear veils or mantels, but a first-century writer tells us that in Paul's native Tarsus women were dressed so that "nobody could see any part of them" and they themselves "could not see anything off the road" (Dio Chrysostom, *Or.* XXXIII 48). It is this kind of conventional dress which Paul advo-

cates. How does he do it? By arguing like this: (a) women
are at the bottom of the hierarchy God-Christ-husband-
wife, and unless they wear veils they put their husbands to
shame in some unexplained way. (b) A woman without a
veil is like a woman without hair; the latter is "shameful"; so
is the former. (c) Men do not wear veils because they are
images of God. The first woman was made from the first
man, so women ought to wear veils. They ought to be veiled
"because of the angels," too. At this point Paul's arguments
apparently seem oppressive even to him, and he adds some
remarks about the mutuality of the sexes and the divine
origin of both. But then he returns to his idiosyncracy. (d) Is
it suitable for a woman to pray unveiled? (The answer to this
is surely Yes.) (e) "Does not nature itself teach us that if a
man has long hair it is a disgrace for him, while if a woman
has long hair, it is her glory? And her hair was given her for
a covering." This argument is the strangest of all. Certainly
"nature" teaches nothing of the sort, and even if it did, one
could hardly prove the need of veils in this way; rather the
contrary. (f) So finally we come to tradition, and it turns out
to be church convention. "If anyone thinks of being argumentative, we have no such custom, nor do the churches
of God." That is to say, the churches of God with which Paul
was acquainted. One can hardly suppose that he checked on
this "tradition" by making a survey.

Our esteem for tradition in the Pauline churches can
hardly be strengthened from 1 Corinthians 11, at least in
the part dealing with women's wearing of veils. What Paul
turns to next, however, has proved to be far more meaningful to later Christians and presumably was more meaningful to him, too. This is the question of the Lord's Supper as
observed at Corinth. In dealing with the Supper, and explaining that it is not to be taken as just an ordinary meal,
Paul explicitly refers to the tradition which, he says, he

"received from the Lord" and "delivered" to the Corinthians. Since it is unlikely that Paul, who was not present at the Last Supper, received such a tradition "from the Lord," exegetes have suggested either that he is speaking of "the Lord" as the ultimate source of the words spoken or that by "the Lord" he means "the tradition." It seems more likely that had he meant to speak of tradition as such he would have done so, and I think he means simply that the Supper was originally the Lord's and the words were especially his. The tradition is this:

> ... that the Lord Jesus, on the night when he was betrayed, took bread, gave thanks, broke it, and said, "This is my body, which is for you; do this in remembrance of me." Similarly the cup after supping, saying, "This cup is the new covenant in my blood; do this, whenever you drink it, in remembrance of me."

Then Paul continues without a break into his own interpretation: "For whenever you eat this bread and drink the cup, you proclaim the death of the Lord until he comes" (11:23–26).

Exactly the same features are present as the ones we found in looking at the tradition about divorce and remarriage. First, Paul is making use of a saying already interpreted in the tradition. In the accounts of the Last Supper provided in the synoptic gospels, we find the command to repeat the breaking of the bread only in the longer version of Luke 22 (19b, perhaps even derived from First Corinthians). It is almost certainly a liturgical addition, made in conformity to the actual Christian continuation of cultic meals (cf. Luke 24:35; Acts 2:42). In Paul's tradition the command to repeat has been used in regard to the bread and has been extended to the cup. Second, Paul feels free to draw inferences from the tradition and to present them

without interruption, almost as if they were part of the
tradition itself: "you proclaim the Lord's death." Of course,
you proclaim the Lord's death, for the giving of his body
and the covenant in his blood were completed on the cross.
But the formulation is Paul's own, one would assume.

In the fourteenth chapter of this letter, we find another
significant passage, even though the word "tradition" does
not occur. As so often, Paul is giving orders to the Corinthians, and again in regard to women. First he appeals once
more to general church usage. "As in all the churches of the
saints, women are to be silent in the churches; for they are
not permitted to speak; they are to be submissive, as the law
also says" (14:34). Church custom, plus a vague allusion to
the story in Genesis about how Eve was to turn to her
husband. But there is more. "If they want to learn anything,
they are to ask their own husbands, at home; for it is shameful for a woman to speak in church" (14:35). The word
"shameful" puts us on the alert. This is the same kind of
term used at the end of the argument about veils. We might
almost be hearing about what is "suitable" and what "nature
teaches." The answer to Paul's implicit question is this: no, it
is not shameful for a woman to speak in church. Perhaps
anticipating some such comment, he goes on to ask the
Corinthians, "Did the message of God come forth from you,
or reach you alone?" The answer to both questions is, of
course, No, but Paul's unstated presupposition, that therefore women cannot speak in church, is completely untena-
ble. And now, at the end of this section, we find his ultimate
authoritative appeal. "If anyone thinks he is a prophet or a
'spiritual,' he must recognize that what I write to you is a
commandment of the Lord. Whoever does not recognize
this is not recognized" (14:37–38). This kind of argumentation is just what we found at the end of the chapter on
divorce and remarriage. Paul finally states that his own
conclusions are based on a divine gift. There he said that he

possessed the Spirit. Here he says that his command is the Lord's command. In other words, his interpretation of the common tradition is also the tradition. One would have expected this conclusion, for he repeatedly states that the gospel is his gospel and that there is no other (Gal. 1:6–9; 2 Cor. 11:4).

Thus far in First Corinthians, some of the passages about tradition have proved disappointing, others rewarding. The most rewarding of all comes last. This is the passage in the fifteenth chapter in which Paul deals with the apostolic tradition about the death and resurrection of Christ. At the very beginning of the chapter, he identifies it with "the gospel" and calls it the means of salvation.

> I delivered to you as of primary importance what I too had received: that Christ died for our sins in accordance with the scriptures, and that he was buried, and that he was raised on the third day in accordance with the scriptures, and that he appeared to Cephas, then to the Twelve, then to more than 500 brothers all at once (most of whom are still alive, though some have died); then he appeared to James, then to all the apostles; last of all, he appeared to me as to someone insignificant.

Obviously a tradition, obviously all-important, obviously already interpreted, and indeed formalized; note that both death and resurrection are "in accordance with the scriptures." Then come two clusters of resurrection appearances, headed first by Cephas (i.e., Peter), next by James. Finally, "last of all," comes Paul himself and his role in relation to the earlier tradition. One may doubt that at Jerusalem they spoke much about the appearance to Paul, and the book of Acts does not treat it as a resurrection-appearance at all. But for Paul and the interpretation of his gospel that he gives to his churches this was the final vision. Probably one should not say "climax," for Paul does have some feeling of his own inadequacy: "I am the least of the apostles, unworthy to be called an apostle, for I persecuted the church of God."

In spite of his weakness and unworthiness, he insists upon his personal place in the gospel, in the resurrection, in the whole story of redemption. "By God's grace I am what I am [i.e., an apostle] and his grace towards me was not in vain, but I worked harder than all of them—not I but the grace of God with me" (15:1–11). Just as in earlier instances of Paul's use of tradition, so here he appropriates it, relates himself to it, speaks of God's grace or spirit, gives the tradition of his own interpretation.

Now if we go back over the various traditions of which Paul has spoken in this letter, we find a few that have to do with conventional behavior and impress one as not unlike the rabbinic-type interpretations which Jesus himself rejected. They have to do with such trivial matters as women's wearing veils or keeping silence in church. They have rather more to do with Paul's prejudices than with his gospel. Then there are the discussions supposedly based on what the Lord had taught in regard to divorce and remarriage and the support of Christian ministers. These discussions show Paul reflecting on the meaning of situations current in his own churches and trying to solve problems partly in relation to the Lord's words, partly in relation to current ethical thought, and (in the case of the support of ministers) by far-fetched exegetical imaginings. Finally, there are the all-important passages in which Paul appeals to the gospel tradition as delivered to himself. He speaks of the Last Supper and gives its context "on the night when he was betrayed." Obviously, the tradition, though complete in itself, is part of a larger whole, the story of Christ's suffering and death. Again, the tradition about the resurrection appearances begins with Christ's death and burial and therefore has a larger context too.

It is this kind of tradition which, at the time when the only Christian scripture was the Old Testament, was to undergo two modifications: first, it was to be fixed in written form (though in several written forms, actually); second, the written fixed forms were to be regarded as scripture like the Old Testament.

Before we close our discussion of Paul and such traditions we should add one more example, this time from First Thessalonians. First, he states his theological conclusion; then he backs it up with a traditional "word of the Lord." The conclusion is this: "if we believe that Jesus died and arose, so also [we must believe that] God will bring those who have died 'through Jesus' with him" (4:14). Then comes the tradition. "For we tell you this with a word of the Lord, that we who are left alive at the coming of the Lord shall not precede those who have died. For the Lord himself, with a shout, with the voice of an archangel and with the trumpet of God, will come down from heaven, and the dead in Christ will be raised first, then we who are left alive shall be snatched up with them in the clouds to meet the Lord in the air, and thus we shall always be with the Lord. So encourage one another with these words" (4:15–18). The fact that the tradition, if we may call it such, itself refers to "the Lord" does not encourage us to assume that it comes directly from Jesus, who was not accustomed to speak of himself in this way. The elaborate stage machinery is not especially convincing either. "Of that day or that hour no one knows, neither the angels in heaven nor the Son, but only the Father" (Mark 13:32). Perhaps the words are those of some Christian prophet who, like Paul, believed the Lord was speaking through him. There are other examples of such "traditions" in millenarian writers of the second century, and without the preservation of the tradition in writing it was always fatally easy for traditions to be made up.

My purpose in this lecture, however, is not to be negative

about the early traditions, but indeed to insist that during
the first generation of Christian life—say roughly from 30
to 70 A.D.—the core of tradition was essentially coextensive
with the gospel. The kinds of questions that vex us today
obviously could not arise. For a Christian there could be no
question about "scripture or tradition," for the scripture
was the Old Testament, which was viewed as largely pointing toward Christ, and the tradition was primarily the gospel. In part, the simplicity of thought in this period was due
to the fact that the extreme tensions and variations which
we find in the second century and later had not yet arisen.
The church was a new movement, not quite so prone to
conflict as it would be later. There was a note of urgency
about presenting the gospel everywhere at once, or at least
throughout the Roman empire.

What happened to oral traditions after Paul's time? Some
of them, of course, were put into written form. Not all, of
course: John 21:25 states that "there are also many other
things which Jesus did; were every one of them to be written, I suppose that the world itself could not contain the
books that would be written." We shall deal more explicitly
with the written gospels in our next lecture. Here we are
concerned with the survival of the oral. Helmut Koester has
presented strong arguments for the use of oral traditions by
most of the so-called Apostolic Fathers in the early second
century.[3] Though not all the evidence he cites seems equally
convincing, no one can finally *prove* that the earlier Apostolic Fathers used books. Is there any way to prove absolutely that one is misquoting a book and not quoting an oral
tradition? Or vice versa?

Certainly one author explicitly discussed the oral traditions and valued them highly. This was a bishop of
Hierapolis in Phrygia, named Papias, who lived in the late
first century or the early second. What we know about him
comes from two early Christians who sharply disagreed

about his merits. Their disagreement takes us toward the heart of the problem about tradition in the early period. Papias himself firmly believed in the coming of the kingdom of God on earth. He believed that there would be a time of miraculous fertility when grapes, wheat, and other plants would produce enormous crops for human consumption, while all the animals would be tame. Such an expectation, obviously based on statements by the Old Testament prophets and by Jewish apocalyptic writers, had been set forth by Jesus himself, in Papias' view.[4] We cannot tell whether Papias was right or not, since our gospels contain so little explicit teaching of Jesus about life in the kingdom of God. It is enough to say that the church father Irenaeus of Lyons, writing at the end of the second century, accepted this testimony and described Papias as an "ancient man" who had been taught by John, the Lord's disciple.

When the fourth-century church historian, Eusebius, began writing about Papias he accepted what Irenaeus had said about him. But as he went on working at the *Church History,* he came to the conclusion that Papias' statements about the kingdom of God on earth were theologically and politically unsound. As Eusebius finally decided, the closest that Christians were likely to come to the reign of God, at least in his lifetime, would be the reign of the emperor Constantine. He therefore undertook further study of Papias' writings, and he found that there was an ambiguous statement at the beginning of them. When Eusebius completed the last edition of his *Church History,* he took Papias' ambiguous language and argued that all his traditions came to him from the followers of the apostles, not from the apostles themselves.

What had happened was that in the ongoing life of the church views like those of Papias became obsolete. Whether or not the early disciples of Jesus expected the kingdom of God to come immediately, as Luke (19:11) says they did, by

the fourth century, when Eusebius wrote, such ideas were
no longer widely acceptable, and this kind of tradition was
therefore criticized and, if necessary, suppressed.

Around the same time as Papias, others whose traditions
were even less palatable to ordinary Christians were telling
how they had received them. The Gnostic teacher Basilides
claimed that he had been instructed by a mysterious
Glaucias. Papias had said that Mark had been an "interpre-
ter" or translator for Peter; Basilides claimed that Glaucias
performed the same function for the same apostle. Similarly, another Gnostic teacher named Valentinus said that
his own teacher had been Theodas, a disciple of Paul. Apparently Valentinus had in mind the more normal tradition
that it was Luke who was Paul's disciple and, like Mark,
wrote a gospel.[5] And Valentinus' own disciple Ptolemaeus,
perhaps about 160, said that his Gnostic group had received
its "apostolic tradition" by "succession," just as ordinary
Christians claimed to have received theirs.[6] In such an era
of claims and counterclaims about tradition it was inevitable
that more emphasis would come to be laid on the written
word and on the collecting of acceptable books.

When we find traditions about what Jesus taught handed
down by the Gnostics and finally written in their books, they
do not strike us as possessing any claim to authenticity.
There is no reason whatever to assume that either among
the Gnostics or their opponents traditions would be reliably
maintained for a century or more. Memory does not serve
that well. Moreover, the Gnostic teachings of Jesus are
usually close to the Gnostic myths, which it is hard to imagine Jesus really taught.

For this reason, the books created and handed down by
more ordinary Christians seem generally more reliable and
closer to the events of the apostolic age. It is sometimes
claimed that in a book like the Gospel of Thomas, primarily
though not entirely Gnostic, some traditions about the

teaching of Jesus are preserved as reliably as in the canonical gospels. Theoretically, this is possible. Since the norm of what Jesus actually taught must be sought within the canonical gospels, however—notably in the synoptics or rather, their sources—it is hard to see how a gospel like Thomas could provide anything new or different. Almost by definition a novelty would have to be rejected.

Christian writers at the end of the second century, and a few even later, quote sayings of Jesus from unwritten tradition. Some of them could be genuine. But the problem of certifying oral tradition became overwhelmingly difficult. Sometimes we imaginatively create a simple pastoral society in which pious men (women, too) would be occupied with little more than meditating on the Lord's words and handing them down. There are at least two difficulties with such a fancy. First, to meditate on the words would certainly mean distorting them. Within days or weeks, not years or decades, the meditation would have replaced the words. Second, Christianity did not arise or grow in a simple pastoral society. It lived and spread in big cities not unlike our own. The tradition that survived was the tradition preserved in books, especially the canonical books.

One of the best attested bits of so-called tradition in early Christianity is the rather cryptic saying, "Become approved money-changers." The point of the saying presumably is that approved money-changers can tell the difference between genuine and false coins and they give correct weights and exchange rates. In the Christian context, they can differentiate authentic and nonauthentic traditions. Which is this?

If we look simply at how widely the saying is cited by early Christians, we may be tempted to suppose that such attestation proves something. But suppose we look more closely. At Alexandria, Clement quotes it as "scripture," while Origen not only does the same but also calls it a commandment of Jesus. In spite of these witnesses, two later Alexandrians ascribe it to Paul. In the west, both Caesarius of Arles and Cassian of Marseilles think it comes from a gospel; so does the second-century Marcionite Apelles. In various pseudo-apostolic apocryphal works it is simply called traditional ("it was said"). The confusion over its origin does not really commend it as genuine. This example, probably the strongest, does not encourage belief in authentic traditions circulated outside the New Testament books.[7]

Clement of Alexandria highly valued that traditional saying of Jesus. Here is another he provides for us. "The Lord said, 'He who has married is not to cast out his wife and he who has not married is not to marry.' "[8] The only place in the New Testament where you can find anything like this is in First Corinthians, and it certainly does not come from Jesus. This shows again how dangerous the notion of ongoing oral tradition can be.

One more statement by the church historian Eusebius will show us how dangerous the notion of tradition, unchecked by written documents, could be. Eusebius describes the letters of Ignatius of Antioch, and tells us something about their content. He says that Ignatius urged the churches of Asia Minor "to cling closely to the tradition of the apostles" and he wrote his letters to the churches because he thought it necessary, "for safety's sake, for the tradition to be given a fixed form in writing."[9] This is an interesting hypothesis. But there is no warrant whatever for it in Ignatius' own letters, which, as it happens, have been preserved. Indeed, his letters do not contain the words "tradition," "safety," "fixed form," or "in writing." Eusebius' picture of Ignatius as his own kind of traditionalist comes from his imagination. This is the danger we encounter if we exaggerate the importance of oral tradition after the early years of the first century.

Notes

1. A. Adam, *Texte zum Manichäismus* (Berlin, 1954) text 3, lines 30–38.
2. R. M. Grant, *The Letter and the Spirit* (London, 1956) pp. 62–66.
3. *Synoptische Ueberlieferungen bei den Apostolischen Vätern* (Berlin, 1957).
4. Fragment in Irenaeus, *Adv. haer.* V 33, 3–4.
5. Clement of Alexandria, *Stromata* VII 106, 4; cf. Hippolytus, *Ref.* VII 20, 1.
6. Ptolemaeus in Epiphanius, *Haer.* XXXIII 7.
7. A. Resch, *Agrapha* (ed. 2, Leipzig, 1906) pp. 112–28; cf. J. Jeremias, *Unknown Sayings of Jesus* (New York, 1957) p. 92; J. Finegan, *Hidden Records of the Life of Jesus* (Philadelphia-Boston, n.d.) pp. 132–33.
8. Clement, *Stromata* III 97, 4.
9. Eusebius, *Hist. Eccl.* III 36, 4.

CHAPTER TWO

From Tradition To Scripture and Back

Robert M. Grant

What the enigmatic title of this lecture means is simply that it will discuss the creation of written documents, later called scripture, and the gradual development of fairly clear traditions concerning the ways to interpret the old documents (the Old Testament) and the new ones. Actually, all such titles are misleading for at least two reasons. First, it is much harder than you might suppose to say when or how new elements were added to the traditions or even to the writings of a vigorous religious movement like early Christianity. Second, we have rather less information about first-, second-, and even third-century Christianity than you would think from looking at all the modern books about the early church. But in spite of these difficulties something can be said.

In the first lecture, we saw the apostle Paul making use of earlier traditions, especially in his first letter to the Corinthians. Obviously such letters were saved; perhaps he saved copies himself. Presumably not all the churches to which he wrote kept his letters. Some may have been trivial even though apostolic; others may have been even more irritating to the recipients than, we may suppose, Galatians was. The letters were obviously apostolic. But until the conception of scripture developed in the church they were not scripture. For the earliest churches the only scripture was the Old Testament.

By the time of Paul's death, in the latter years of the emperor Nero, some of his most important letters were still available in various localities; we do not know whether or not small collections were in circulation. The decade in which he died was extremely important in relation to the New Testament. Other apostles also died, and it became clear that they were not surviving until the coming of the reign of God which Jesus had proclaimed. Two conclusions, both important for Christian life and literature, were drawn. First, the reign of God as announced by Jesus was not going to come immediately. There would be a much longer period of waiting and of Christian mission than the apostles had at first supposed. Therefore, it would be important to have written documents containing apostolic and postapostolic traditions and interpretations. Second, if the books were in some way to be apostolic they should be written while the memory of the apostles was still present at least among their disciples.

In consequence of this situation, what seems at first to have existed only as oral tradition—the story of Jesus' death and resurrection, and the compilation of his teaching—was given the kind of framework which we find in the Gospel of Mark. It was Mark, perhaps a disciple of Peter, who created the gospel "form," a form which immediately proved highly satisfactory to Christian preachers and teachers and led finally to the creation of three more examples, ascribed to Matthew, Luke, and John.

We need not enter into the details of the creation of any of the gospels. For our purposes it is sufficient to note that the problem of how to interpret the gospels may not have been acute when Mark, for example, was present to explain what he meant. But it reached a critical stage within a generation. It is most unlikely that the authors of Matthew or Luke or John expected readers to use Mark in addition to any one of the later gospels, or any other than a single one of the later gospels. The modern study of "redaction criticism" emphasizes the theological intentions of each of the evangelists, and some of these intentions are almost certainly mutually exclusive. Each evangelist was convinced that his own interpretation of the mission of Jesus was the right one. We can see this especially clearly when we notice how Matthew and Luke rewrote Mark.

The problem of New Testament interpretation grew up with the collecting of the New Testament books. If at Corinth Christians had one or two of Paul's letters and maybe one gospel, they did not have insuperable exegetical problems. It is when they got two or three gospels that trouble really arose. This was the problem that Marcion of Pontus tried to solve by keeping only one gospel, Luke, and cutting it down to theological size by leaving out whatever did not agree with his collection of Paul's letters.

My point here is this: the rise of a specifically Christian literature solved some problems, for the main outlines of the gospel were now fairly well fixed, not to say preserved; but it raised many more problems, especially because of the divergences among the gospels and between them and the epistles. Marcion solved the problem very neatly, by simply rejecting much of the Christian tradition and what was to be the Christian scripture. According to Irenaeus of Lyons, it was characteristic of heretics that they took only a part of the evidence. The Ebionites or Jewish Christians used only Matthew; Marcion took Luke; Docetists, who separated "Christ" from Jesus, used only Mark; Valentinian theosophists liked John.[1] Again, the followers of Marcion said that only Paul knew the truth of revelation.[2]

The church generally preserved and interpreted the four canonical gospels ascribed to apostles (Matthew, John) or their disciples (Mark, Luke). In a Roman Christian document of about 160, we hear of the gospels as compositions of the apostles and their followers; and a statement found in Mark is ascribed to "the memoranda of Peter."[3] At this point, however, nothing was made of the disagreements to be found among the books. These disagreements came to present severe difficulties to many Christians. In Asia Minor and at Rome there were those who talked about the obvious disagreements between John and any one of the synoptic gospels, and some who tried to remove both the Gospel and the Apocalypse ascribed to John from among the writings approved by the church as a whole. Again, there were more practical-minded persons who argued about the right time for terminating the Good Friday fast. Were they to follow the chronology set forth in Matthew or the one provided in John? What was to be done under such circumstances?

Irenaeus, bishop of Lyons in Gaul, presented the view accepted by most. He held that the true interpretation of the scriptures was to be found among those who had received the apostolic tradition along with the apostolic succession, and possessed the charismatic gift of truth.[4]

True "gnosis" is the teaching of the apostles, and the ancient structure of the church throughout the world, and the form of the body of Christ in accordance with the successions of bishops to whom the apostles delivered the church which is in each place; this teaching has come down to us, preserved without any use of forged writings, by being handled in its complete fullness, neither receiving addition nor suffering curtailment; and reading without falsification, and honest and steady exposition of the scriptures without either danger or blasphemy; and the special gift of love. . . .

Love is presumably mentioned because without it exegetes are likely to disagree even more than they would with it. Irenaeus' picture seems idealized, since there was actually considerable diversity among both writings and exegetes. But in his view one had to escape from the Gnostics by fleeing for refuge to the church, being brought up in her bosom, and being nourished by the Dominical scriptures. The Gnostics, he says, exaggerate the importance of the intellect and condemn the inexperience of the holy presbyters.[5] Such words might suggest that Irenaeus did not value the role of intelligence in theology. Actually, however, he was simply trying to defend the presbyters against what he regarded as the instability and blasphemy of the Gnostic teachers.

Some Christians, he says, actually do have more intelligence than others. They should use it not to create Gnostic heresy but to investigate theological questions within a context; they should "work out the truth of those things spoken in parables and assimilate it to the 'hypothesis' of faith." By "hypothesis" Irenaeus does not mean the traditional baptismal creeds or even local rules of faith. He means the basic structure of Christianity, underlying scripture, tradition, creeds and rules.[6] By "those things spoken in parables" he means whatever is expressed in figurative language or whose meaning is not immediately apparent. What the Christian teacher does with these materials and others is to work out and correlate problems related to God's plan of salvation. Thus, he will consider such matters as God's patience with angels and men, his creation of varieties of beings (temporal/eternal, heavenly/earthly), his appearing to men under different forms, his giving several covenants and placing all under sin so that he could have mercy on all (Rom. 11:32), and finally matters related to the incarnation, the church, and the resurrection. This passage presents Irenaeus' plan for an exegetical theology.

We should beware of reading more into such a statement than really belongs there. The intelligent Christian Irenaeus had in mind was actually himself. He was the theologian of his time who, above all, was interested in exactly the questions he lists, and he set forth answers to them in the course of his treatise against heresies. There is what we may call a universalizing style about all the ancient theologians. Perhaps it is not confined to the ancients. In spite of the necessary limitations we must place around his remarks, it remains true that his statement was influential. We shall see something like it picked up by Origen. Doubtless it commended itself because Irenaeus was trying to define the relation between scripture and tradition and to leave room for the exercise of a Christian's intelligence.

Irenaeus frequently speaks about the exegesis of the parables of Jesus and of other mysterious and difficult sections of scripture. He severely criticizes the Gnostics for laying so much emphasis on these sections, as well as for disagreeing among themselves as to what they mean. The scriptures contain perfectly clear teaching about the one God and his creation of the universe. Instead of building on the rock of plain teaching, they build on the sand of ambiguities. It is true, Irenaeus admits, that solutions of all the problems presented by the scriptures cannot be given. However, he argues, contemporary science does not solve all problems either. We need not be ashamed to confess that we do not know what God was doing before he made the universe, for scripture does not tell us. It is better to admit our ignorance than to invent a series of emanations, as the Gnostics do. The Lord himself said that "of the final day and hour no one knows, not even the Son, but the Father alone" (Mark 13:32); and the Apostle wrote, "We know in part, and we prophesy in part" (1 Cor. 13:9).[7] Clarity, simplicity, and modesty should serve as guides in exegesis.

Two examples will show how the exegetical method of Irenaeus worked. First, he compares the composition of Gnostic gospels and other writings to the weaving of ropes out of sand. The Gnostics take little grains of apostolic tradition and move them around just enough to keep them recognizable while altering their meaning. Another way to put it, he says, is to compare their work with that of someone who takes a fine mosaic portrait of a king, made of precious gems, and uses the stones to produce a mosaic of a dog or a fox. When he claims that it is the original portrait of the king, he can actually deceive inexperienced viewers.[8] Anyone who has looked at the Gnostic Gospel of Thomas will recognize what Irenaeus is talking about. Here is a collection of the words of Jesus, partly taken from a canonical gospel, partly just invented, with the whole providing the impression that Jesus was a Gnostic teacher and redeemer.[9]

In discussing the Gnostics' rearrangement of the stones in the mosaic, Irenaeus says that they "destroy the underlying notion of a man," apparently the notion presented to the mind of the mosaic-maker, whom Irenaeus calls "the wise artisan." Such a description of the mosaic-maker recalls Paul's words in 1 Corinthians 3:10–15. There the Apostle pointed to the unity of the apostolic preaching as like a building erected on one foundation, Jesus Christ. As a "wise builder" Paul laid this foundation and others were able to build upon it either with gold, silver, and precious stones, or with wood, hay and straw. Irenaeus has kept the ideas of a foundation and of precious stones. He has substituted a more general picture for Paul's precise words about Jesus Christ as the foundation. But this point must be the same as Paul's. There is one basic meaning to the scriptures, and it comes from the authentic picture of Christ as handed down by the apostles. The Gnostics may maintain a different "hypothesis," but the prophets did not proclaim it, the Lord did not teach it, and the apostles did not hand it down.

A little later he makes the same point again, using a different analogy. In his time, rhetoricians and others amused themselves by stringing together isolated verses from the *Iliad* and the *Odyssey* and creating so-called Homeric poems. Irenaeus insists that a person who is "acquainted with the Homeric 'hypothesis'," i.e., with the basic outline and content of the Homeric poems, will restore the verses to their original contexts. And when he explains what he means by his analogies (he refers back to the mosaic), he explicitly defines the Christian equivalent to the king's portrait or the true Homer.[10]

> So he who maintains the rule of truth within himself without deviation, the one which he received through baptism, will recognize the names and the expressions and the parables taken [by the Gnostics] from the scriptures but will not accept their blasphemous "hypothesis."

Our second example is not so satisfactory. Irenaeus was much impressed by the traditions handed down in Asia Minor, and from certain "elders" he had picked up the notion that Jesus's mission lasted until he was nearly fifty years old. The elders claimed that the fact was proved in John 8:57 when Jesus was asked, "You are not yet fifty years old, and have you seen Abraham?" If Jesus had been about thirty, it would have been said that he was not yet forty.[11] Regrettably, Irenaeus took this all very seriously, and in consequence, in his *Demonstration of the Apostolic Preaching*, he had Pontius Pilate governing Judaea under the emperor Claudius so that the chronology would be improved.[12]

To say this is not to claim that Irenaeus' exegetical work was entirely mistaken or valueless, especially in his own time. It is to say that the synthesis he endeavored to create and preserve, against the Gnostics' searches for antithesis and analysis, was not really broadly enough based. It found unity prematurely. It did not sufficiently allow for the diversity to be found in the scriptures and within the Catholic tradition. His comparison of the portrait of Christ in the gospels with a mosaic is not so much based on the gospels as it is on his own synthetic understanding of the gospels. He minimizes their differences and insipidly compares them with four beasts in the Apocalypse of John.[13] The Gospel of John, then, is like a lion, for it speaks of divine rule and authority. Luke is sacerdotal because a calf is sacrificial. Matthew is human. Mark is like an eagle, spiritual. This artificial construct shows that Irenaeus had not thought much, if at all, about the actual differences among the gospels.

For the relation between scripture and tradition, the most important passage in Irenaeus' work occurs at the beginning of his third book. There he echoed what Clement of Rome had said about apostolic tradition and succession; there he spoke of the origins of the four gospels and about their unanimous teaching. He pointed out that heretics were opposed first to the scriptures and then to the tradition. He therefore believed it necessary to vindicate the tradition as held in succession from the apostles, and as his prime example he chose the episcopal succession of the Roman church. The Roman church, he argued, was "most ancient, known to all, and founded and established by the two very famous apostles Peter and Paul." The words with which Irenaeus further justified his appeal to Roman precedent have been matters of controversy for centuries. The most likely translation is given in the latest edition of the text, and in English it reads thus: "for with this church, because of its superior origin, every church must necessarily be in agreement, i.e., the believers from everywhere; this church in which always, for the benefit of those who are from everywhere, has been preserved the tradition which is from the apostles."[14] This is to say that Roman tradition is reliable because of its apostolicity and antiquity, which (in Irenaeus' opinion) must result in the *consénsio* of all Christians everywhere. He then traces the Roman episcopal succession up to his own time, summarizes the content of the

Roman letter First Clement (perhaps with Second Clement also), and speaks again of "the most ancient churches" and the agreement (*adsensus*) even of barbarian Christians with them, as contrasted with the novelty of heresies.[15]

If we ask how such arguments would be understood in the Graeco-Roman world in which Irenaeus lived, we can find excellent parallels in the philosophical works of Cicero. These parallels are valuable not because Irenaeus had ever read a line of Cicero's writings but because Cicero reflected the philosophical and semiphilosophical currents of the late republican and early imperial ages so well. What we evidently have in Irenaeus is a Christianized version of the argument from antiquity, as related to universality, which is found, for example, in Cicero's *Tusculan Disputations*. The Latin orator, giving a historical proof of the immortality of the soul, argues first that belief in the gods was shared by "all antiquity," next that "there is no nation so fierce that . . . belief in the gods has not inspired it." In Cicero's opinion "the consensus of all is the voice of nature"; this means that one must consider the views of "all who are everywhere."[16] Similarly, at the beginning of his treatise *On Divination* he speaks of "the ancient opinion derived even from the times of the heroes and confirmed by the consensus of the [Roman] people and all nations.[17] The resemblance of such doctrines to those expressed by Irenaeus is obvious. What the Roman church, in his view, is maintaining is the true Christian view, not just because it is Roman but because it is ancient and apostolic and also universally acknowledged.

At the other end of the Mediterranean world, Clement of Alexandria was providing teaching remarkably like that of Irenaeus. He spoke of the "rule of truth" as a sure criterion for differentiating true and false; it came from "the truth itself," i.e., from Christ, and was commended by "the church tradition." When Christians use the criterion, they "obtain a perfect proof concerning the scriptures from the

scriptures themselves." Thus, they necessarily oppose heretics, who do not follow this usage. The heretics use only
some of the scriptures, or only parts of various books. They
do not interpret them in relation to the "body" and the
"connecting tissue" of the whole. Instead, they rely on ambiguous and isolated expressions and pay attention to
words, not ideas.[18] Irenaeus too had identified the truth
with Christ, and he had made the same criticism of heretical
exegetes.[19] Indeed, Clement's picture of the "body" and the
"connecting tissue" (one might say, "thread of argument")
is much like Irenaeus' "hypothesis" or central meaning
underlying the scriptures.[20]

We should not dissociate Christian exegesis from the
world in which it arose. The principle of contextual interpretation was nothing new. The philosopher Porphyry
wrote several studies of Homer in which he did exegesis in a
traditional-grammatical manner, and he spoke of interpreting Homer by Homer.[21] This is the same kind of approach
as interpreting scripture by scripture.

It is important to notice, however, that in spite of Clement's conservative-sounding language he actually did not
hesitate to allegorize both the Old Testament and the gospels. He was convinced, as he said in his address entitled *The
Rich Man's Salvation,* that "the Savior teaches his people
nothing in a merely human way, but everything by a divine
and mystical wisdom." Because this was so, "we must not
understand his words literally."[22] Use of the allegorical
method at Alexandria had been given impetus among
Christians because it had been favored by Hellenistic Jews,
especially by the great Alexandrian teacher Philo. And in
the writings of the Alexandrian Christian Origen, a generation after Clement, it provoked fresh enthusiasm and criticism. The enthusiasm was due to Origen himself and his
disciples, who believed that by allegorizing the scriptures
they were recovering their true meaning. The criticism was

provided by such a later author as Vincentius of Lerinum (to whom we shall return). In Vincentius' view, Origen's "new manner" of interpretation was due to his "despising ecclesiastical traditions and the doctrines of the ancients."[23] This was not Origen's own view of what he was doing. And in the first pages of his treatise *On First Principles* he tried to show what areas in Christian tradition permitted further exploration and, indeed, required it.

One almost hears an echo of Paul's "I say, not the Lord" when one looks at Origen's discussion of what the apostles taught and did not teach.[24] In his view they definitely laid down the main lines of Christian doctrine, the "necessary doctrines." What they did not set forth, however, was the justification or analysis of the doctrines in relation to philosophical theology. This study was reserved for a later time, especially for those to whom the Holy Spirit would impart the spiritual gifts of language, wisdom, and knowledge—in other words, for theologians.

Origen explicitly states what the necessary doctrines are. First, of course, comes the doctrine of the unity, transcendence, creative activity, and redemptive acts of God. Second is the traditional—as developed in the course of the second century—teaching about Christ Jesus and his birth, death, and resurrection. Third is the doctrine of the Holy Spirit, "united in dignity with the Father and the Son." Here Origen explicitly states that there are matters for investigation: is the Spirit created or uncreated? Is he a Son of God? This is, he says, "not yet clearly known." The apostles also taught that the soul will receive rewards and punishments because it possessed free will; but there is no definite doctrine about its origin. The church teaches that the devil and his angels exist, but the nature of their existence is "not explained very clearly." The world was made and will dissolve, but there is no clear statement about what came before and what will come afterwards. There is also the doctrine of scripture, to the effect that the scriptures were composed through the Spirit and contain two meanings. In every case, the theologian can construct a connected body of doctrine out of these primary points. He draws conclusions of a logical nature from the axioms.

In other words, he creates a philosophical theology. It is very important for us to notice that this is exactly what Origen himself does. And he does so by relentless use of the allegorical method, to which he devotes the last book of his treatise *On First Principles*. First he argues from the scriptures that there are at least two meanings in biblical texts. Then he proceeds to show what the content of the hidden meaning is. We are not surprised to learn that this content consists of the answers to the questions he himself raised in his preface.[25]

It is obvious that Origen draws no sharp line, at least here, between scripture and tradition. The apostolic preaching or teaching is the basic matter, and this is what the church also preaches and teaches. Theologians do not change what the apostles taught but simply fill in the logical gaps. Indeed, Origen explicitly says that such is the case. "The teaching of the church, handed down in unbroken succession from the apostles, is still preserved and continues to exist in the churches up to the present day," and therefore "we maintain that that only is to be believed as the truth which in no way conflicts with the tradition of the church and the apostles."[26] The successors of the apostles work out the implications and thus (though Origen does not use the term) doctrine develops.

It may be that Origen is not absolutely frank in his discussion of this subject. It is likely that when he gives Christian traditions a Middle Platonic setting he has really altered not only their logical interconnections but, in some measure, their substance. But it is hard to see how theology could ever arise unless risks like this were taken and unless some modification actually did occur as the traditions, in writing or not, were reinterpreted for varying circumstances.[27]

In the early third century Origen was not the only Christian writer to be aware of the way in which the church had moved beyond reproducing the exact circumstances of the apostolic age. At Carthage the vigorous rhetorician Tertullian made a similar observation in regard to the church's liturgical practices. He was arguing that church custom did not need to be derived from scripture, and he listed items observed on the ground of tradition alone. Some had to do with baptism, such as, renunciation of the devil, immersion as threefold, a developed baptismal creed, the use of milk and honey, and the avoidance of bathing for a week after baptism. Some were eucharistic, such as, celebrations before dawn, reception of the elements only from presbyters or the bishop, and annual celebrations in memory of the dead. In addition, there was to be no fasting or kneeling on Sundays or between Easter and Pentecost; consecrated bread and wine were not to fall on the ground; and the sign of the cross was to be employed often during the day.[28] We might suppose that such matters were less significant than the theological developments allowed for by Origen. But in the history of Christianity liturgical matters have often reflected life styles and existential concerns even more than theology has. To change the time of the eucharist from evening to dawn obviously involved thought, discussion, and decision, if not conflict. Other points were no less important.

Tertullian certainly shows that in the third century one *could* claim the primacy of tradition over scripture. He does not show that it was a good idea, for he brings these matters up only in order to show that Christian soldiers ought not to wear crowns at military ceremonies. It has not been customary for Jewish Christians to wear crowns. Therefore, on the ground of tradition, and also on the ground that crowns are unnatural, no one should wear them. It is hard for us to be very enthusiastic about this line of thought.

Furthermore, as Hanson points out, in a later work Tertullian took exactly the opposite approach.[29] Should women who have vowed to be perpetually virgins wear veils or not? The church custom was that they should not. Tertullian disagreed with the custom. He violently attacked custom and appealed both to scripture and to the (written) oracles of the Montanist prophets. (This was in his treatise *De virginibus velandis*.)

The contradiction suggests that one cannot take Tertullian altogether seriously when he insists too much on the primacy of tradition or, again, on the primacy of scripture. The ultimate authority must surely have been what lay behind both scripture and tradition, the apostolic gospel.

It is well known that Tertullian tried to cut the ground from under his opponents by an appeal to legal practice. In Roman law there was such a thing as a *praescriptio*, or demurrer, often related to the competence of a plaintiff to bring suit. Obviously, if the plaintiff was not competent, the suit as such did not need to be argued. So it is that Tertullian claims, in his treatise *De praescriptione haereticorum*, that the heretics cannot be allowed to present arguments based on the scriptures. First, the apostolic churches possess the truth given them by the apostles; the heretics disagree among themselves and therefore do not possess the truth. Second, the church's teaching is chronologically prior to that of the heretics; it is true while theirs is false. Finally, the scriptures are the property of the church. The heretics are trespassers on the church's land. Obviously the three arguments really boil down to one: the scriptures belong to the church and no one outside can interpret them.

No "heretic" worth his salt would have let Tertullian get away with this kind of argument, and it is not surprising that he had to write long argumentative treatises in which he set forth his exegesis of scripture. In several of them he referred to his "prescription" argument,[30] but in each case he kept right on arguing as if he had not mentioned it. Did he even take it seriously himself?

For later times the most important patristic discussion of scripture and tradition was probably the one provided before the middle of the fifth century by Vincentius, a monk of Lerinum or St. Honorat. In his view, the ultimate doctrinal authority was scripture, "the divine law," interpreted in the light of "the tradition of the Catholic church." The tradition is necessary, he held, because of the diversity of the opinions held by exegetes. "The line of prophetic and apostolic interpretation should be directed in accordance with the norm of the ecclesiastical and Catholic understanding." To discover what this is, we must look for "what has been believed everywhere, always, by everyone." The appeal is to "ecumenicity," "antiquity," and "consent" or "consensus" (*consensio*).[31]

This famous rule is of course easier to state than to apply. Vincentius himself seems to have been trying to use it against Augustine's views on predestination. He criticizes earlier African Christians like Tertullian and, though very cautiously, Cyprian. He quotes Stephen of Rome as having said, "No innovation except what is handed down," and treats this as a general principle favoring antiquity against novelty.[32] At the same time, he admits that development (*profectus*) has to take place; but it must not be alteration (*permutatio*).[33]

In the case of Vincentius the dependence on Graeco-Roman models, of which we spoke in regard to Irenaeus, seems definitely assured. He plainly relies on Cicero when he writes that he would rather be wrong with Origen than right with others. Cicero had said the same thing about Plato—and in just the section of the *Tusculane* where he was dealing with antiquity and consensus.[34] It is virtually certain that Vincentius' ideas are traditionally classical as well as traditionally Christian.

Again, when Vincentius appeals to the past, he is not imagining that every Christian's judgment was equally valid. Instead, he refers to "the holy fathers" and their *consensio*. This, as Pease pointed out, has its analogy in the Ciceronian practice of appealing to the agreement of philosophers rather than of people in general.[35] But Vincentius was not so unrealistic as to suppose that the tradition actually was unanimous. The *consensio* he wants followed is that given by "the definitions and judgments (*sententiae*) of all, or nearly all, the bishops and teachers."[36] Even with this modification, which points in the direction of majority decisions, the trouble with the rule is that it is essentially unhistorical. It does not take into account historical conditioning in scripture itself or among the transmitters of tradition. And in actual practice it usually involves simply neglecting or condemning those with whom the majority disagree. In Vincentius' own time forgery flourished to an astounding extent as theologians tried to prove that their own opinions had really been held by Christian writers in the second century. For a long time thereafter the documents supposed to represent early tradition were the products of fourth- and fifth-century controversy.

Does this mean that scripture must be open to the inspired or not so inspired interpretation of anyone who claims the ability to interpret it? More probably, the tradition of the church generally considered can continue to provide general guidance insofar as it, like scripture, is based on the gospel. To think that there is only one possible line of biblical interpretation or of theology, however, would seem to involve repeating the errors of earlier times.

Notes

1. *Adv. haer.* III 11, 7.
2. *Ibid.*, III 13, 1.

3. Justin, *Dial.*, 103,8; 106,3; cf. R. M. Grant, *The Formation of the New Testament* (London, 1965) p. 135.

4. *Adv. haer.* IV 26,2; 32, 2; 33,8. Translation of the last with the aid of R. P. C. Hanson, *Tradition in the Early Church* (London, 1962) p. 95.

5. Irenaeus, *Adv. haer.* V 20,1.

6. *Ibid.*, I 10, 3. Cf. P. Hefner, "Theological Methodology in St. Irenaeus," *Journal of Religion* 44 (1964) pp. 294–309; N. Brox, *Offenbarung, Gnosis und gnostischer Mythos bei Irenäus von Lyon* (Salzburg, 1966) esp. pp. 106–13.

7. *Adv. haer.* II 27–28.

8. *Ibid.*, *Adv. haer.* I 8, 1.

9. Cf. R. M. Grant—D. N. Freedman, *The Secret Saying of Jesus* (London, 1960).

10. *Adv. haer.* I 9, 4.

11. Irenaeus, *Adv. haer.* II 22, 5–6.

12. Irenaeus, *Epideixis* 74.

13. *Adv. haer.* III 11, 8.

14. Irenaeus, *Adv. haer.* III 3, 2: A. Rousseau—L. Doutreleau, *Irénée de Lyon, Contre les hérésies, Livre* (Paris, 1974), II 32–33; cf. I, 112–36.

15. *Ibid.*, III 4, 1–3.

16. Cicero, *Tusc. disp.* I 26–29; 30–35.

17. Cicero, *De div.* I 1 (cf. 11); cf. A. S. Pease, *M. Tulli Ciceronis De Divinatione Liber Primus* ([Urbana,] 1920) p. 39.

18. Clement, *Stromata* VII, 94–96.

19. *Adv. haer.* II 28, 1; 26, 2.

20. Irenaeus too speaks of "body of truth" in regard to the true meaning of scripture (*Adv. haer.* I 9, 4). Cf. Hanson, *op. cit.*, p. 109, n. 6.

21. References in G. Wolff, *Porphyrii De philosophia ex oraculis haurienda* (repr. Hildesheim, 1962) p. 17.

22. Clement, *Quis dives salvetur* 5.

23. Vincentius, *Commonitorium* XVII (23).

24. Origen, *De principiis* I praef., 3–9.

25. *Ibid.*, IV 2,7 (cf. 3, 15).

26. *Ibid.*, I, praef. 2.

27. On the extent to which Origen's theology did break fresh

ground there has been virtually unending debate. Perhaps the most important recent discussion is by F. H. Kettler, *Der ursprüngliche Sinn der Dogmatik des Origenes* (Berlin, 1966). In an address at the Patristic Conference in Oxford (1971) Cardinal Daniélou cited it with approval; cf. *Nouvelle revue théologigue* 94 (1972) pp. 460–61.

28. Tertullian, *De corona* 3, 1–4; cf. R. P. C. Hanson, *op. cit.*, pp. 131–33.

29. *Ibid.*, 133–36.

30. List in D. van den Eynde, *Les normes de l'enseignement chrétien dans la littérature patristique des trois premiers siecles* (Gembloux-Paris, 1933) p. 202, n. 4.

31. *Common.* I–II.

32. *Ibid.*, V, (9). Apparently Stephen was referring only to the imposition of hands on penitent heretics; cf. Cyprian, *Ep.* 74.

33. *Ibid.*, XXIII (28).

34. *Ibid.*, XVII (23); Cicero, *Tusc.* I 39.

35. A. S. Pease, *M. Tulli Ciceronis De Natura Deorum* (Cambridge, Mass., 1955) pp. 294–95.

36. *Common.* II (3).

CHAPTER THREE

Christian Tradition and the Early Middle Ages

Robert E. McNally, S.J.

Christian tradition in the Early Middle Ages was woven into the very substance of life.[1] It formed Christianity and was inseparable from it. Tradition was not merely a matter of theology or of epistemology; its principal concern was the social and the spiritual more than the academic and the theoretical. It was basically religious; and in a very important way it was also cultural—the principal provider of the foundation stones of civilization, as it was then known. Tradition, therefore, in the medieval context was universal, encompassing God and man, pope and emperor, lord and vassal; it established *sacerdotium* and *imperium,* presided over *studium,* regulated matter and spirit, and it even canonized the saints. Tradition divided and explicated history; it founded world chronology; it named the months and the days, and it marked out the planets and the stars that were believed to be decisive in mankind's destiny. Medieval man was born according to nature, but he died according to tradition. Apart from it there was nothing important in his life. Writing from another point of view a recent playwright put it this way: "Tradition! Tradition! A man without tradition is as shaky as a fiddler on the roof"—words which

37

epitomize in a bizarre way the medieval comprehension of the tradition on which life was formed and structured.

For the early medieval man tradition was the cultural medium, the spiritual atmosphere, the religious climate in which he was born, lived, and died. It was as connatural to him as water to a fish; for it provided the basic sustenance which nourished his spirit. It was a lifeline connecting him with Christian antiquity, with the ultimate source, therefore, of that goodness, truth and beauty that formed his life-ideal. In the thinking of the Early Middle Ages the culture of the ancient world was a center of gravity and a model to be imitated. Union with Rome, the antiquity of Rome, even the idea of Rome were antidotes against the death of the world which was keenly sensed on all sides.[2] The unknown author of an early medieval *florilegium* that has come down to us under the name of Bede stated his conviction of the relation of Rome to the survival of the world in these words:

> As long as the Colosseum stands, Rome also stands;
>   When the Colosseum falls, then Rome falls;
>   When Rome falls, the whole world falls.[3]

It would not be easy to find a more succinct and pointed way of emphasizing the sustaining power of ancient tradition. The mystique of Rome, of *Roma nobilis* as the poet sang, was a powerful inspiration in early medieval life.[4]

The medieval world was a distinctly Western and Latin phenomenon deriving its strength and character from the *Geistesgut* of antiquity. It is pertinent to the valid comprehension and evaluation of medieval tradition to appreciate the extent of its dependence on the intellectual and spiritual riches of the past. But the mere possession of this inheritance does not by itself fully explicate or exhaust the meaning of the relation of this tradition to its cultural and historical origins. Present is a further element—a feeling of inferiority face to face with antiquity and a genuine desire to be elevated by it. In this ancient culture medieval man saw new horizons opening to him; herein his insights were clarified and his understanding deepened. In its attitude to its origins the Early Middle Ages was open, benign, tolerant; it was ready and willing to be influenced, formed, and finally transformed by the past. But this readiness to be educated by the cultural ideals of antiquity is a vital force in the anatomy of tradition in the Early Middle Ages. It inspired, in fact it sustained, medieval man's tireless quest of the ancient world.

Medieval man perceived himself in almost a mystical relationship to the historical past. It was a matter not merely of transcribing history but of transforming it, sharing in it, and even being absorbed by it. Augustine's interpretation of the meaning of the trilingual suprascription of the Cross of Christ is rich in the light that it throws on the character of this perception. John notes in his gospel (John 19: 19–20); "Pilate wrote a title and put it on the cross; it read: 'Jesus of Nazareth, the King of the Jews'.... It was written in Hebrew, in Latin and in Greek." Augustine explains the text in this way:

These three languages are eminent above all others:

Hebrew, because of the Jews who glory in the law of God; Greek, because of the thinkers among the Gentile nations; Latin, because of the Romans who hold sway over many and over almost all peoples.[5]

This explanation of the three languages of the Cross was preserved and transmitted by the Middle Ages.[6] In accepting the Cross of Jesus Christ one accepted not only the primacy of Hebrew, Latin and Greek, the languages which in a universal way proclaimed the kingship of Christ, but also the historical, cultural and religious realities which their cosmic symbolism simultaneously revealed and concealed; for buried beneath them is the world in which tradition was conceived and born.

On the basis of Augustine's interpretation of these Johannine texts certain corollaries were derived that contributed in an important way to the formation of the medieval mind and its comprehension of tradition. Hebrew, Latin and Greek were enhanced with a mysticism that made them the *tres linguae sacrae:* Hebrew, the language of Jerusalem; Greek, the language of Athens; and Latin, the language of Rome.[7] This way of understanding the Johannine texts led logically to further symbols—to Jerusalem as the city of revelation, to Athens as the city of wisdom, to Rome as the city of law; that is, to Christ, to Plato, and to Caesar. But the basic concepts underlying these groups of languages, cities and persons allowed for expansion into other triads, for example: theology from Jerusalem, philosophy from Athens, law from Rome; and, finally, *sacerdotium, imperium* and *studium*—papacy, empire and university—as the three foundation stones on which the fabric of the whole world was believed to rest. *Sacerdotium* belonged to Italy; *imperium,* to Germany; and *studium,* to France. The approach was characteristically medieval in its attempt to relate the current world to its distant historical origins.

The early medieval question was not whether there were separate and distinct fonts of revelation, scripture, and tradition; nor was it, in other words, whether tradition contained revealed truths that were not to be found in scripture. This formulation of the problem was the product of late medieval thinking; it was studied by the theologians of the fifteenth century, came to fullness in the following century, and is a classical example of Trent's reaction to the Protestant problematic of the day.[8] The early medieval understanding of tradition was simple, direct, and unsophisticated. It was not the center of apologetics or of polemics; nor was it the object of study or speculation. Face to face with Christian tradition there was admiration, wonder, and appreciation. For to the early medieval mind tradition was fundamentally and simply the truth of the Christian religion transmitted as a corpus. It was the deposit of God's revelation; it was the teaching of Jesus Christ.

Tradition was not only this living doctrine; it was also the mode in which and through which it passed from generation to generation. Early medieval man did not consider scripture and tradition as two separate and distinct receptacles in which God's revelation was preserved and through which it was transmitted. The church read scripture as its book.[9] Its exposition of the sense of the sacred text was its word. It was the perennial word of the church expressing its understanding of the kerygma. This, then, is tradition—the gospel read in the context of the church, interpreted by the church and passed on by the church through the ages. It is not surprising that in the Early Middle Ages tradition was not adequately distinguished either from church or from scripture. When the church explained the sense of scripture, which it had read, it unfolded and handed on the tradition which it had received. Tradition, therefore, was objective, ancient and sapiential; but above all else it was churchly.[10]

The medieval world rested on the authority of Christian antiquity, especially on the legacy of the Fathers of the church. This is a valid generalization; but lest it be exaggerated, let the following points serve as correctives: (1) Greek as a literature was not an immediate, formative influence on the West. The scholars who had a mastery of this language in the Early Middle Ages numbered no more than four or five persons. The tradition of Greek Christianity was, therefore, not directly accessible to the Latin Middle Ages. What was known of the religious thought of the Eastern Church was transmitted partially in translations, citations and paraphrases; the West had no comprehensive grasp of its theology or liturgy. (2) Because of the depressed state of culture in the first part of this period not all the works of the Latin Fathers were known; and all too often the texts which were on hand were defective, incomplete, and isolated. For example, no library at the time contained the complete corpus of Augustine, and no scholar until Anselm of Canterbury (d. 1109) comprehended Augustine's thought as a theological system. The problem of tradition in the Early Middle Ages, therefore, was principally concerned with the influence of the Latin Fathers on the religious experience of the new nations that were to form Western Christendom. (3) The traditions that interested the early medieval church were more properly religious than theological. This was understandable in view of the fact that the spirit of the age was more pastoral than academic, more involved in missionary enterprise than in theological controversy. Concretely, this means that among the prime sources for studying the concept of tradition in the Early Middle Ages are homilies or sermons preached in the context of worship. They are of the kerygmatic order and, in consequence, they frequently reflect the direct influence of patristic thought, though rarely, if ever, in its purest and most complete form.[11]

The spirit that animated the process of handing on tradition was conservative, restrictive, and exclusive. It echoed Paul's advice to the Thessalonians (2 Thess. 2:15): "So then, brethren, stand firm and hold to the traditions which you were taught by us, either by word of mouth or by letter." Its negative aspect is summed up in the baptismal canon of Pope St. Stephen I (d.257): "Nihil innouetur nisi quod traditum est."[12] ("Let there be no innovations save on the basis of tradition.") And as the baptismal order was regulated and controlled by the ancient discipline of the church, so the faith was formulated and explicated to conform to its perennial profession. Yesterday's belief is today's faith, and tomorrow's faith is today's belief. It parallels the sense of the text (Heb. 13:8): "Jesus Christ is the same yesterday and today and forever." The preoccupation was to transmit the tradition that represented the kerygma of the ancient church and that was believed to be dogmatically pure. Its response to the words of Paul (2 Tim. 1:14): "Guard the truth that has been entrusted to you by the Holy Spirit," was effective and affirmative. That was the ideal; it was a stubborn, persistent, static one. Its positive aspect is epitomized by Martin Grabmann in two words, *Rezeptivität* and *Traditionalismus.*[13]

This Christian tradition, which was normative for the magisterial function of the church, was expressed in creedal statements, conciliar decrees, canon law and various works of art, in paintings, mosaics, statues, book illuminations, but especially in the writings of the Fathers of the Church. These were renowned Churchmen of the past, known for their pure orthodoxy, their great antiquity, and their conspicuous sanctity. Their literary productions, representing their preaching and teaching, were received by the church with special reverence and trust because they were thought to express the heart and soul of the revelation entrusted to it by Christ himself. The character of the witness which they rendered within the church made their works monuments to the faith. The *Decretum Gelasianum* dating from the early sixth-century Upper Italy prescribes among other things that "the works and treatises of all the orthodox fathers should be read, fathers who in no wise deviated from communion with the Roman Church nor separated from its faith and preaching, but shared in communion with it through the grace of God even up to the last day of their lives."[14] This way of speaking about the Fathers of the Church would become typical of the Early Middle Ages.

Tradition showed what the faith was; it also showed what the faith was not. Tradition was living and it was ancient, and it opened up for the Christian the principal point of entrance into the ancient world. Concretely it was embodied in the legacy of the Fathers. As we have seen, Greek was effectively excluded because of the lack of philological expertise. The Latin Fathers, most influential as preservers and transmitters of Christian tradition, were Ambrose, Jerome, Augustine, and Gregory. By the beginning of the eighth century the four had coalesced into a fixed tetrad: they were *the* Fathers of the Latin Church. They were without peer. They were *auctores* who evolved into *auctoritates*. To cite them was to cite authority. Their writings were decisive for the acceptance of this or that dogmatic proposition or liturgical practice as part of the deposit of faith, and in the early medieval period their prestige was truly impressive. The honor and the respect accorded to them are in evidence on all sides.

The Fathers not only established the sense of scripture, but they also defined the hermeneutic in virtue of which this sense was found and verified. Exegesis was the quest for a simultaneous multiplicity of senses—an understanding of the *sensus biblici* which ultimately derived its inspiration and architectonic from Origen. His concept of the biblical senses rested on a comprehension of human nature which was fundamentally neo-Platonic. As man consists of soma, psyche and pneuma (body, soul and spirit), the bible contains somatic, psychic, and pneumatic (literal, moral, and allegorical) senses. This hermeneutic providing for a triad of senses was subsequently transmitted to the Latin West where it was expanded into a tetrad—the literal or historical, and the spiritual or mystical senses, which latter in turn included allegory, tropology, and anagogy. This approach to the exegesis of the sacred text remained standard in the West throughout the Middle Ages and even beyond them.

To say that the Fathers defined biblical hermeneutic is virtually the same as to say that tradition defined it. In fact, the hermeneutic which we have described here came at the end of the Middle Ages to be regarded by some theologians as divinely revealed, a Catholic truth and, therefore, a matter of faith.[15] It is understandable that no one dared to interpret the meaning of the *sacra pagina* in a sense contrary to tradition as contained in and expressed by the patristic *auctores*. In the principal theological controversies of the Carolingian age the prime arguments in favor of the orthodoxy of the church's teaching rested on the Fathers.[16] They occupied a privileged position within the magisterium of the church that no other group enjoyed in the same way and to the same degree. In their pages the echo of God's voice could be heard, and their teaching represented, if not determined, the doctrine of the church at this or that point in its history. Thus the second council of Nicaea (787) in its definition on sacred images (Actio VII, Oct., 13, 787) equivalated the teaching of the Fathers (sanctorum Patrum nostrorum doctrina) and the tradition of the church (traditio sanctae Ecclesiae). This way of talking about the Fathers merely followed an ancient and common usage. Later the expression, "sanctorum patrum exempla sequentes," became relatively ordinary (e.g., C. Lateranense I, can. 1, March 27, 1123) as a succinct expression of the antiquity and the authority of tradition.

The principal preoccupation of the early medieval exegetes was the discovery and the reproduction of the scriptural interpretations of the Fathers. Thus we have the evaluation of Beryl Smalley: "To study the commentaries of Alcuin, Claudius of Turin, Raban Maur, and Walafrid Strabo, his pupil, to mention outstanding names, is simply to study their sources."[17] But it is precisely these sources which contain and express the Christian tradition that was received from the past and transmitted to the future. The medieval mind believed that the key that opened the ultimate meaning of the sacred text was the patristic interpretation. It not only shed light on textual obscurities, but it also yielded an authoritative exegesis in conformity with the Catholic faith. And in this sense the medieval man believed that he was closely related to revelation, to God's word and God's thought. This strong inclination to bible study was responsible to a considerable degree for the preservation of patristic literature, and it contributed to the progressive development of theology as biblical exegesis.[18]

Tradition performed valuable services for theology; it guided the theologian to revelation, sustained and directed his research of it, provided a basis for theological reflection and helped to maintain a balance between old and new. But tradition of itself was not theology; it did not solve the intellectual problems that may have arisen from the profession of the faith. It did not open avenues and vistas of new thought nor did it pose original questions; it provided, however, a firm epistemological foundation for theology, since it imported the authority of the church itself. In this early period theology was more religious than scientific; it was oriented more to the preservation of truth than to its creation; it looked more to the past than to the future. Since theology coincided with biblical exegesis, theology was in a sense the pursuit of tradition.

Throughout the Early Middle Ages theology was largely monastic, not only in its central purpose or function but also in its essential method and appeal. In the period before the foundation of the cathedral schools and the great universities theology was written by the monk for his monastic community. According to his way of thinking theology was neither abstract nor academic. It was rather a religious experience, a personal quest, the discovery and possession of God as both object and subject of love. The monk was devoted more to the pursuit of the good than of the true; he was concerned more with the acquisition of love than knowledge. His theology presented a spiritual doctrine more than a rationale of revelation. He was neither critical nor problem-conscious, and the tenor of his mind inclined him to tradition, to reverence and absorb it into the fabric of his own religious life.[19]

For the monk, the perennial problem of his vocation was the relation of monasticism to its first origins and the discovery there of its true spirit. Thus the evaluation of tradition opened the way to the establishment of a valid principle whereby the monk could personally identify with his own history. In the prescriptions of the night office the *Regula Sancti Benedicti* (c.9) commends the reading of the biblical commentaries of the distinguished and orthodox Catholic Fathers; and elsewhere in the *Regula* the monks are exhorted to search out the origins of their traditions in the writings of the Eastern Fathers, the celebrated monks of the desert, whose lives coincided with the primordial stages in the origins of monasticism. Thus the monastic commitment to tradition (to the traditions of *ecclesia* and *regula*) prepared the monk for theology in an atmosphere defined by *traditionalismus*.[20]

In order to appreciate the character of tradition in the Early Middle Ages it is to be remembered that the inner structure of society at that time was monolithic. There was faith in one God, one Lord, one Christ and one church. There was only one tradition, according to which the believers held on to what they had received from those who went before them. There was no dogmatic or religious pluralism. There was only unity, harmony, and concordance in matters of faith, and heresy was rare. Consequently there was no external competition between tradition and tradition, just as there was no on-going dialectic between theology and theology. Thus there was no need of apologetics within the Christian community. This, of course, reduced tension among the faithful and strengthened the appeal of the kerygma to nonbelievers.

How the faith was professed at this time is illustrated by Gregory of Tours (d.594). In the beginning of his *Historia* he confesses openly his Christian faith, and he declares that despite certain technical or stylistic errors that mar his work it is his sole desire to adhere without error to the church, to its faith and to its preaching because that is the way to win forgiveness and salvation. Thereupon he sets down the creed as his witness to his orthodoxy and as proof of his participation in its traditions. There is here a marked simplicity and directness; salvation is conceived as flowing from a firm adhesion to the Catholic church and to its ancient, apostolic traditions.[21]

For the monastic theology of the Early Middle Ages the testimony of tradition was indispensible for opening the sense of Holy Scripture and for marking out the dimensions of the Christian mysteries. The witness of tradition was accepted without question, for it was a privileged and a decisive authority whose prestige derived from its acceptance by the church as a deposit of revelation. The history of the Easter controversy that rocked insular Christianity in the seventh century offers a classic example of how in the dialectic of tradition universalism prevailed over particularism; it shows how the tradition of the universal church displaced the tradition of a particular church, how Roman usage finally set aside Celtic usage.[22]

Two groups of Christians—Celts and Saxons—living side by side in the British isles, in what is now northeastern England and southeastern Scotland, disagreed in their determination of the date of the annual observance of Easter. The historical origins of the differences and their religious meaning are obscure; they involve, however, more than chronological niceties. Two different paschal tables were used in their calculations, and each table rested on what was believed to be an "apostolic" tradition. The presupposites underlying the two methods were distinct from one another. The Saxons maintained that they were in the tradition of St. Peter; the Celts in the tradition of St. John. The former followed the usage of the Roman church; the latter, the usage of the Celtic church. Which tradition should prevail? Which tradition was more authentic, more ancient, more pure? The problem here was neither dogmatic nor theological; it was more procedural, more a question of church order and discipline, but it involved highly sensitive religious issues. It is worthy of consideration here because it is the kind of controversy that has haunted the church from earliest times. How is the authentic tradition to be discerned when each contending party to a theological dispute believes that its position alone derives from apostolic origins?

It is an elementary point of medieval history that the celebrated Paschal Controversy was resolved at the Synod of Whitby (664). The debate described for us by Bede took place in the presence of the great Northumbrian king Oswiu and the principal lords of both church and kingdom. Appropriately the point of contention was defined by the king as the quest for "the truer tradition" (*verior traditio*). St. Colman (d. 677), the leader of the Celtic party, presented the Irish position as resting on the authority of St. John, on the paschal table of Anatolius, and on the approval of St. Columba. In response the Roman-minded St. Wilfrid (d.709) dramatically urged the usage of the Catholic church as the norm for determining the date of the observance of Easter. "For," he said to the Irish, "though your fathers were holy men, do you think that a handful of people in one corner of the remotest of islands is to be preferred to the universal church of Christ which is spread throughout the World?" And he concluded: "Is that Columba of yours . . . to be preferred to the most blessed chief of the apostles. . . ?"[23] The argument was decisive. King Oswiu put aside John's tradition in favor of Peter's; he accepted the Roman usage as "the truer tradition" and, therefore, as the

tradition to be followed; it rested on the supreme and
apostolic authority of the head of the apostles whom he was
unwilling either to offend or to disobey, but it also represented the style and practice of the universal, Catholic
church.

The fact that tradition was left unquestioned, unassailed,
and unchallenged allowed it to harden into a mould that
restricted its flexibility and, therefore, its efficacy. But more
than that, the increment of patristic literature in the
Carolingian renaissance through the discovery of hitherto
inaccessible works, the correction of ancient texts, the tran-
scription of new manuscripts, and the mutiplication of
library holdings provided theology with problems that had
no immediate solution. At times, the citation of patristic
authorities (and, presumably, therefore of tradition itself)
involved theological proof in verbal and factual error, in
textual contradictions of the first order. Instead of being an
illumination, tradition had become obscure, confused, and
uncertain. The problematic was serious: first, it directly
touched Christian tradition, its preservation and communi-
cation; and, second, it concerned religious authority which,
after all, is useful and valid only to the extent that it is
reasonable, coherent, and consistent. Clearly this growing
disorder in the sources of tradition could cause theological
crisis, for Christianity cannot thrive, or even survive, if its
inner truth does not rest on a secure foundation.

It is to the credit of Abelard (d.1142) that he had the
courage, the intelligence, and the insight to address himself
to the textual problem of tradition, a problem which, if left
unresolved, would distort Christian theology, certainly im-
pede, if not destroy, its development. Yet that is the direction in which the unreconciled traditions of Christianity
were leading the church. Problems that voluntarism might
have induced monastic theologians to overlook or suppress
posed a challenge to the intellectualism of the new theology

of the twelfth century. The story of Abelard's career is well known through his own candid self-revelations. On a personal or social level he was a difficult character, proud, arrogant, vain, overbearing, and unyielding; but intellectually he was perceptive, independent, critical, inventive, and penetrating. His mind was sharp in a distinctly Celtic way. Thus, by disposition he was well suited to face the hard questions which the decrepit sources of tradition were posing.

The problems were complex. First, in Abelard's day there was on hand no articulated, accepted theology of tradition; and second, there was no well established scientific method for justifying the theological sources of tradition. Textual criticism was virtually unknown. It played no role in the old monastic theology and it was not part of the intellectual equipment of the new scholasticism. To underscore the character of the problem which confronted the sources of tradition, Abelard arranged side by side various patristic and biblical *sententiae* which ostensibly differed from one another and in some cases seemed even contradictory. The evidence, as it stood, pointed to ominous conclusions. It touched on 150 important theological matters, and it posed manifold questions: Does the tradition of the church, as transmitted in the historical sources, repudiate and contradict itself? In consequence, is there a valid Christian tradition? Can there be a viable, credible Catholic theology?

The problem here arises not only from a certain intellectual disposition, restless with historical sources that lack the discipline of law and order, but it also and especially arises from the quest of the medieval theologian for a *consensus Patrum* to give authority to his biblical exegesis. That a veritable *consensus Patrum* in scriptural and theological questions should be possible, even at times necessary, flowed from the common belief that the writings of the Fathers were inspired by the Holy Spirit. Although their works were not considered canonical, they occupied a privileged position that in some respects was analogous to Holy Scripture. Henri de Lubac has rightly observed: "The medieval formulae relative to the harmony of the Fathers of the Church often resemble the patristic formulae relative to the harmony of the scriptures; and the resemblance is such that there is no need to doubt the filiation of the one with the other."[24] Thus as the consent of the Fathers provided proof for the inerrancy and infallibility of Holy Scripture, the consent of the theologians proved an assurance against the errancy and the fallibility of the Fathers. Ultimately it became axiomatic to say that the Fathers, when unanimous in their teaching on faith and morals, were inspired and infallible.[25]

Abelard believed that a method could be devised to preserve the integrity and dignity of Christian tradition by bringing its external parts into harmony with one another. His conception of the problem, while promising and valid, was not totally original. Preoccupied with the verbal and factual discrepancies that in the course of time had crept into the *textus receptus* of the canon law, canonists such as Ivo of Chartres (d.1116) had developed a method for establishing their legal texts. It was to prove influential, imitable and programmatic far beyond the realm of *iura*.[26] Further, there was the important, though less sophisticated, work of Bernold of Constance (d.1100), who undertook the solution of the same kind of textual problems that were to engage Abelard some decades later.[27] As theology gradually developed from the monastic to the scholastic, it was seriously beset by the problem of the historical value of the sources of Christian tradition. This was to prove the greatest threat to the credibility of tradition until the reformation of the sixteenth century.

The rules which Abelard set down were simple and direct, in a sense almost obvious. If tradition were created in time, transmitted in words and preserved in manuscripts, then the method that studied it should be prepared to handle problems posed by history, philology and dialectic. The result was the highly important work that has come down to us under the title *Sic et Non*.[28] Here rules were formulated to demonstrate the credibility of tradition. Abelard wished to show that the contradictions and discrepancies discernible between various texts were only apparent, and that by the application of a rigorous method the textual conflict could be mitigated, if not simply resolved. To certain of his contemporaries Abelard's approach seemed scientific and rationalistic; in their eyes it involved the submission of divine revelation to clinical autopsy; it was shocking, therefore, irreverent and irreligious. It was an unjustified criticism inspired by the fact that Abelard was considered to be the inventor of a *theologia noua* at direct odds with the traditional theology of the church.[29]

The introduction of Abelard's method into the study of historical theology obviously did not settle all the problems which the sources posed. That may have been partly due to the very character of the texts, but it may also have been due to the problems themselves and manner in which they were presented. Too often the controverted texts were simply juxtaposed to bring out the reality of the discrepancy between them; they were rarely treated organically, in terms of their genesis. The result was a reconciliation of texts that tended to be artificial and contrived. Interest centered more on the text than on the context. Still Abelard's method did clarify certain issues, and ultimately in the hands of his followers it broadened the perspective of what might be called patristic theology. Obscurities remained. No amount of dialectical manipulation could bring everything into harmony. There was always something left over that could not be reconciled. Here the adage already ancient even in Abelard's day was applied to the Fathers—*Diuersi, non aduersi.*[30] Patristic thought contains within itself what is diverse, not what is adverse. Its external differences are compatible with its internal harmony.

If scripture tells us what God's word is, tradition explains what God's word means. Bible study is a vertical experience, not because God's word comes down from on high, but because this word from on high is fathomless; its profundity is deep beyond measure. Near the end of his *Confessions* (XII,xiv,17) Augustine put it this way:

> Wondrous is the depth of your words whose surface delighting your little ones stands before us. But wondrous is their depth, O my God, wondrous is their depth. It is awesome to look into that depth; it is an awe owed to honor and it is a trembling arising from love!

And this conviction, this outpouring of Augustine inspired by a sudden, clear perception of the wonder and the majesty of scripture, its breadth and its depth, runs as a thread through the biblical literature of the Middle Ages. Scripture is a well, a pond, a stream, an ocean finally, but without any discernible depth. Its sense is without limit and without measure. If theology and exegesis coincide (as indeed they did in the Middle Ages), then as exegesis has no limit neither does theology. The quest of God never ends because there is no end to his self-revelation in scripture.

If the study of scripture was a vertical, downward experience, the study of tradition was a horizontal, outward experience; the pursuit of scripture was intensive; the pursuit of tradition was extensive. A depression of tradition was apt to render exegesis sterile; its exaggeration would make it unnecessary. How could medieval man be tradition-minded, yet be progressive and forward thinking? If he concentrated on the future, he would be in danger of neglecting the past; yet if the past were unduly consulted, the present might well be ignored. Did medieval man need two heads so that he could simultaneously look backward and forward? Was he able to walk to the right and to the left at the same time?

Early medieval man did not think in categories such as these. From the twelfth century there are extant statements that illustrate in a metaphorical way the concordance between past and future, between tradition and progress. It is not surprising that this way of thinking emerges in the circle of Chartres whose learned life exemplifies so beautifully the cooperation of old and new in the quest of wisdom. Peter of Blois (d. ca.1200), who may have been a disciple of John of Salisbury, described in a letter to Reginald of Bath the relation of past and present in these words:

> We are like dwarfs standing on the shoulders of giants; thanks to them, we see farther than they. Busying ourselves with the treatises written by the ancients, we take their choice thoughts, buried by age and the neglect of men, and we raise them, as it were, from death to renewed life.[31]

The metaphor was well known at Chartres and even beyond the walls of its celebrated school.[32] Its message was clear: no man is isolated in his search for knowledge and understanding. Even the illustrious saints of God knew that truth, a truth that the great rose window in Notre Dame of Chartres proclaims so magnificently. Here we see high up on the southern wall Isaiah, Zechariah, Jeremiah, and Daniel, the four major prophets of the Old Law, standing in a blaze of glory; and we see further Matthew, Mark, Luke, and John, the four evangelists of the New Law, straddling like dwarfs the backs of these famed giants and gazing intently over their shoulders into the distant future. This is an awesome way of representing what every medieval man recognized who beheld the sight—that tradition like a mystical thread runs through all history, accumulating, preserving, and transmitting its spiritual values; that civilization without forsaking its past moves onward to the future; and that through the past the shape of the future becomes discernible to the present.

Notes

1. Over the years since 1962 a vast literature on the relation between scripture and tradition has accumulated. Cf. for some of the more important titles Yves M.-J. Congar, "Le débat sur la question du rapport entre Ecriture et Tradition au point de vue de leur contenu matériel," *Revue des sciences philosophiques et théologiques* 48 (1964) pp. 645–57.

2. Columbanus (d.615) expressed the eschatological spirit of his day in his *Carmen de transitu mundi* this way: "Mundus iste transibit, / Cottidie decrescit; / Nemo uiuens manebit, / Nullus uiuus remansit. / . . . ." His sustaining hope, however, is not Rome but Christ. Cf. G.S.M. Walker, *Sancti Columbani Opera, Scriptores Latini Hiberniae* 2 (Dublin, 1957) pp. 182–83.

3. This curious work without manuscript tradition probably dates from the late eighth century and from insular (Irish?) circles. Cf. PL 94.543B.

4. Cf. F. Schneider, *Rom und Romgedanke im Mittelalter* (Munich, 1926), pp. 1ff., and F.J.E. Raby, *A History of Secular Latin Poetry in the Middle Ages* 1 (Oxford, 1934) p. 291.

5. *In Iohannis Euang.,* c.19, *Tract.* CXVII. 4, *Corpus Christianorum* 36. 653.

6. Cf. the Augustinian tradition in Pseudo-Bede's *Collectanea* (PL 94.547D). The same tradition is reflected in St. Thomas' exegesis of the Johannine texts in his commentary on John's gospel cited by P. Spicq, *Esquisse d'une histoire de l'exégèse latine au moyen-age* (Paris, 1944) p. 182, n.3.

7. Cf. R.E. McNally, S.J., "The 'Tres Linguae Sacrae' in Early Irish Bible Exegesis," *Theological Studies* 19 (1958) pp. 395–403. Cf. on the general problem of Greek in the Early Middle Ages Bernhard Bischoff, "Das griechische Element in der abendländischen Bildung des Mittelalters," *Byzantinische*

Zeitschrift 44 (1951) pp. 27–55.

8. Cf. on this question H. Jedin, *A History of the Council of Trent* 2 (St. Louis, 1961) pp. 52–98.

9. Cf., for example, Hugh of Rouen (d.1164) who in his *Dialogus* (PL 192.1206D) remarks of the relation of church to scripture: "Ecclesia legit et tenet." In this context H.de Lubac remarks: "En ces deux mots, suivant la perspective ancienna, tient la règle de foi." Cf. H.de Lubac, *Exégèse médiévale* 1, 1 (Paris, 1959) p. 59. This way of thinking represents a medieval development of the Augustinian appreciation of the decisive role of the church in all that concerns Holy Scripture.

10. Cf. on the churchly element in biblical exegesis H.de Lubac, *op.cit.,* 1, 1, 56 ff.

11. Cf. J. Jungmann, S.J., "Die Abwehr des Germanischen Arianismus und der Umbruch der religiösen Kultur im Frühen Mittelalter," *Liturgisches Erbe und Pastorale Gegenwart* (Innsbruck, 1960) pp. 49 ff.; 58 ff.

12. Cf. H. Denziger and A. Schönmetzer, edits., *Enchiridion Symbolorum* (ed., 32: Freiburg, 1963) no. 110, p. 47.

13. Cf. M. Grabmann, *Die Geschichte der scholastischen Methode* 1 (Freiburg, 1909) p. 179.

14. Cf. E. von Dobshütz, *Das Decretum Gelasianum* (Leipzig, 1912) pp. 38–39.

15. For example, Francisco Toledo, S.J. (1532–96) in his *In Summam Theol. s. Thomae Aquinatis Enarratio* 1: In primam (Rome, 1869) pp. 53–54, taught that the doctrine of the four senses must be held *de fide.* Cf. H. de Lubac, *op.cit.,* 1, 1, 32–33.

16. The patristic expertise of the Carolingian theologians come to the fore both in the Iconoclastic Controversy and in the dispute with the Spanish Adoptionists. Cf. G. Haendler, *Epochen karolingischer Theologie, Theologische Arbeiten* 10 (Berlin, 1958) pp. 109–119; and E. Aman, *L'Epoque carolingienne, Histoire de l'Eglise* 6 (Paris, 1947) pp. 143 ff.

17. Cf. B. Smalley, *The Study of the Bible in the Middle Ages* (Oxford, 1952) pp. 37–38.

18. Cf. M. Grabmann, *op.cit.,* 1,181: "Die Theologie bestand vor allem in Exegese der Heiligen Schrift, die dem Zwecke nach

ein moralisierenden und allegorisierenden Charakter hatte,
der Form nach ein fast ausschliesslich kompilatorisches Gep-
räge an sich trug." Cf. also H. de Lubac, *op.cit.*, 1, 1, 59–60.

19. Cf. J. Leclercq, *The Love of Learning and the Desire of God* (New
    York, 1961) pp. 233–86.
20. Cf. *ibid.*, pp. 111 ff.
21. Cf. *Historia* I, *Praefatio:* "Scripturus bella regum cum gen-
    tibus aduersis . . . prius fidem meam proferre cupio, ut qui
    ligirit, me non dubitet esse catholicum. . . ."
22. Cf. K. Hughes, *The Church in Early Irish Society* (Ithaca, N.Y.,
    1966) pp. 103 ff.; and J. T. McNeill, *The Celtic Churches, A
    History A.D. 200 to 1200* (Chicago, 1974) pp. 109 ff.
23. Cf. *Bede's Ecclesiastical History of the English People,* III.25,
    edits., B. Colgrave and R.A.B. Mynors (Oxford, 1969) p. 307.
    Note also the very pointed remarks of Cummianus on the
    particularism of the Irish Church in his letter to Ségéne of
    Iona and Beccan, cited by K. Hughes, *op.cit.,* p. 107.
24. Cf. H. de Lubac, S.J., "A propos de la lormule: 'Diversi, sed
    non Adverse,' " *Mélanges Jules Lebreton* 2 (Paris, 1952) p. 28.
25. Cf. G. Bardy, "L'inspiration des Pères de l'Eglise," *Mélanges
    Jules Lebreton* 2 (Paris, 1952) 7–26. In the paraphrase of the
    Decretum Gelasianum in the Irish pseudo-Isidorian *Liber de
    Numeris* (ca.775, Southeast Germany) the inspiration of
    Gregory the Great is described this way: ". . . non dico ipsum
    [Gregorium] sed Spiritum sanctum per ipsum locutum fuisse
    et in digitis eius haec scripsisse. . . ." Cf. E. von Dobschütz, *op.
    cit.,* p. 70.
26. Cf. on the influence of canon law on theological method in
    the Early Middle Ages P. Fournier and G. le Bras, *Histoire des
    collections canoniques en Occident depuis les fausses décrétales jus-
    qu'au Décret de Gratien* 2 (Paris, 1932) pp. 334–50; and J.
    DeGhellinck, *Le mouvement théologique du XIIe siècle* (Paris,
    1948) pp. 203 ff.
27. Cf. on Bernold of Constance and his work, *De sacramentis
    excommunicaorum iuxta assertionem sanctorum Patrum,* M. Grab-
    mann, *op. cit.,* 1, 234 ff.
28. PL 178, 1339–1610.
29. Cf. D.E. Luscombe, *The School of Peter Abelard* (Cambridge,

1969), pp. 1 ff.; A. Forest et al., *Le mouvement doctrinal du XIe au XIVe siècle, Histoire de l'Eglise* 13 (Paris, 1956) p. 106, n. 3; and J. DeGhellinck, *op. cit.,* pp. 149–75.

30. Cf., H. de Lubac, S.J., *Mélanges Jules Lebreton* 2, 38; and J. DeGhellinck, *op. cit.,* p. 520.

31. Epist. 92 (PL 207.290AB).

32. It was Bernard of Chartres who put this metaphor into circulation in the first third of the twelfth century. Cf. M.-D. Chenu, *Nature, Man and Society in the Twelfth Century* (Chicago 1968) p. 326, n.43. Cf. also R. Klibansky, "Standing on the Shoulders of Giants," *Isis* 26 (1936) pp. 147–49.

CHAPTER FOUR

Tradition At the Beginning Of the Reformation

Robert E. McNally, S.J.

Over fifty years ago the illustrious Dutch historian of
European culture, Johan Huizinga (1872–1945), described
the fifteenth century as "the autumn time of the Middle
Ages."[1] His study has not been displaced; in fact, it has
survived and has become a classic in its own genre. The
concept of late medieval culture as a harvest imports an
advanced development of its life-forms, their maturation,
perhaps ripeness and even overripeness, and a kind of
paralysis resulting from the fullness of their vitality. They
had evolved as far as their own inner genetic structure
allowed, and they were no longer capable either of maintaining their essential identity or of expanding with further
growth. Historians of the period have vividly described the
character of this exhaustion, fatigue, and climax which
European civilization then experienced. It was a universal
phenomenon that touched almost every aspect of Christian
life in one way or another.

The times were marked with decadence, showing itself in
a general lassitude and weakness of the moral and religious
orders.[2] The signs there of inner decay and corruption are
unmistakable and ominous, and the sense of hopelessness

and helplessness that filled the atmosphere of this century reveals clearly a deep spiritual depression. It was an age of nervous anxiety, and it is not really surprising to learn that at this time the symptoms of social alienation become clear and firm.[3] The religious art of the period illuminates its disturbed character. We note here a preoccupation, first with death as the last cruelty of human life, and second with final judgment as the inevitable epilogue to existence. It is perhaps here that the Late Middle Ages most sharply reveals the depth of its *Angst*. Hieronymus Bosch's (ca. 1460–1516) representation, "The Seven Deadly Sins and the Four Last Things," shows how deeply man sensed the evil of sin, how keenly he felt the scrutiny of God's eternal vigilance, and how totally his life was lived *sub specie aeternitatis*.[4]

In the fifteenth century European civilization was indeed tired; it was not dead, however. It was waning, but it was not dying. It still possessed a wholesome vitality, even creativity, an inventiveness, a daring and a certain originality. The dread Black Death (1348–49) did not kill everyone, and not everything was destroyed by the Hundred Years War (1339–1453). Under a deceptive facade life was hidden, but it was nonetheless real and effective. In many notable respects the fifteenth century was progressive. It witnessed, for example, the invention of the printing press by Johannes von Gutenberg (ca.1396–1468) and the discovery of the New World by Christopher Columbus at the end of the century. But its essential conservatism is shown in the way that it cherished and preserved the cultural patterns which it had received from those who went before.

The Christian religion in the fifteenth century was not weak nor was it ineffectual. It dominated the scene of late medieval life. The liturgical observances which were celebrated in the great places of worship were well attended. People prayed; they heard sermons; they cultivated relics; they maintained the cult of the saints, and throughout the

year they faithfully kept each fast and feast. They knew how
to enter into the spirit of the sacred mysteries which they
honored; their religious joy and sorrow were part of a real,
perceptible experience. Churches were built; hymns were
written and sung, and paintings and statues were made.
The century produced important religious art and theological literature, and it enriched the church with saints who
represented the power and glory of its sanctity. The mind
of the medieval Christian was thoroughly religious, but it
was also ecclesial, formed by the ascetical doctrine and
practice of the church which despite an increasing inclination towards individualism continued to cherish its ancient
heritage. It is here in the hearts and minds of the faithful
that Christian tradition found its most proper refuge and
sanctuary. It is here that it was most cherished and most
honored, and it is here that it can be most profitably
studied.[5]

The cultural temperament and climate of the late
medieval world created the spiritual and intellectual atmosphere in which Christian tradition was preserved, and it
also provided the concrete, historical channel through
which it was transmitted. The experience of passing
through the long centuries of the Late Middle Ages transformed tradition; it may even have distorted its perspective
and its function. There is evidence from this time that the
ancient tradition of the church was beginning to bifurcate
into new traditions, and that in some cases these new traditions were fragmenting into legends; extraneous elements contaminated the purity of its content, and the bonds
uniting it to the kerygma loosened. The problem of tradition arose from its long exposure to the power of history,
which tends to erode the permanent and enduring.

Tradition rests on history; where history is neglected,
tradition is imperiled. At the end of the Middle Ages history
was neglected, and in consequence tradition was imperiled.

This did not happen by chance; it was the end product of a variety of interacting influences not the least of which was the dim view which theologians took of history. For them the ancient conception was still valid that the theologian was exegete, and that the exegete was theologian. In theory at least, theology still claimed that its principal function was to discover the Christian mystery in revelation, to formulate it in comprehensible terms and to render it reasonable to the human mind. It was the vocation of the theologian to grasp and to express the message which revelation heralded. In this task (where there was question of the sacred page) he followed the hermeneutical pattern which Augustine of Dacia (d.1282) epitomized in the well known hexameters:

> Littera gesta docet; quid credas, allegoria;
> Quid agas, moralis; quo tendas, anagogia.[6]

Thus biblical exegesis like divine revelation started with history and terminated in mystery; it began with letter and culminated in spirit; its thrust was forward, from "then" to "hereafter," and upward, from the historical to the eschatological sense of the text. This way of approaching scripture and understanding it was well known to the Fathers and to the schoolmen, but how is it relevant to the problem of tradition?

First, this basic hermeneutic does not repudiate history (or letter); rather it presupposes and builds upon it, but the significance of history within the broad frame of theology remains minor and lowly. It is related to the true sense of the text in the way that the shell of a nut is related to its kernel: a rough, bitter exteriority conceals a smooth, sweet interiority. Second, this hermeneutic leaves tradition fundamentally intact, but it tries to illuminate its content by making explicit what is implicit in scripture, by manifesting what is hidden there, and by discovering and revealing the mystery which is at the heart of the sacred page. This task,

conceived *iuxta analogiam fidei,* was executed without vio-
lence to the privileged character of tradition and its essential continuity with the past. Thus the theologian, as he
strove to grasp the spiritual sense of the text, transcended
the spatio-temporal limitations of history, the cradle of
tradition, for he worked at his best when he worked with
abstract principles. This approach to scripture and tradition was in conformity with the theological method and
mentality of the Late Middle Ages.

The depreciation of history which materialized from the
biblical hermeneutics of which we have been speaking,
finds striking parallels in certain aspects of the spiritual
doctrine which was then current. In the introduction to his
Vita Christi, the Carthusian Ludolf of Saxony (d.1378) sets
down various observations on the manner in which we
should pray to the Christ of biblical revelation. Note, for
example, this observation which to a degree is typical of the
spirit of the work as a whole:

> Do not believe that every word and deed of Christ on
> which we can meditate, has been written down. Now for
> the greater impression [that they will make upon you] I
> will set down here each event inasmuch as it happened, or
> can be piously believed to have happened, according to
> imaginative representations which the mind projects in
> various ways.[7]

This work is relevant here not only because it colored the
spirituality of the last centuries of the Middle Ages but also
because it reflects the trends which were current at the time.

In the above citation from the *Vita Christi,* Ludolf inti-
mates (what he explicates elsewhere) that prayer should
indeed be structured fundamentally on the sacred text, but
he allows and even counsels a further course of action. The
one who meditates on the life of Christ should use his
imaginative powers (*secundum quasdam imaginativas re-*

praesentationes) to construct or reconstruct the biblical text in its fullness. Apart from other considerations, this manner of praying imports or presupposes a mentality that believes that sacred history is not bound by the laws of evidence, for not "every word and deed of Christ on which we can meditate, has been written down." But this tolerance of an extrabiblical source of the life of Christ, a tradition over and above scripture, opened the door to an uncritical approach to the unique place of the bible in spiritual life and to the creation of historically unfounded biblical saga. Holy Scripture at the mercy of uncontrolled religious imagination is capable of begetting distortions that should have no place in sound Christian spirituality. Their passage into authentic tradition was ominous; it contaminated and marred its simplicity and purity, and even altered its subsequent development.

The concept of tradition was not a negligible factor in late medieval theology, even if it was not a burning issue. The theological writings of the fourteenth and fifteenth centuries show such a diversity of thinking in this matter that it is impossible to speak of one well defined and unified school of thought. Heiko Oberman has conveniently divided the theologies of tradition under two general headings: Tradition I: Tradition and scripture are coextensive in content. There is no revealed truth in tradition which is not first found in scripture; and Tradition II: All revelation is contained in scripture and tradition but in such wise that there are certain truths preserved in tradition which are not found in scripture.[8] The theologizing that has revolved around these two comprehensions of Christian tradition and its proper relation to scripture and revelation has left certain fundamental questions without answer. It does not, for example, tell us why there is need of tradition, if all revelation is in scripture; nor does it tell us why there is need of scripture, if tradition equals and even exceeds it. Tradition is a mystery, which cannot be simply resolved. It can, however, be elucidated, if it is studied not only as a theological theorem but also as a religious phenomenon.

John Brevicoxa (d. 1423) in his excellent treatise, *De fide et ecclesia* ("On Faith, the Church, the Roman Pontiff, and the General Council"), written in the late fourteenth century, allowed for a broad inclusive concept the tradition as a source of revelation. He stated his position on the relation of scripture and tradition this way:

> ... There are many truths to which one ought to assent as a necessary condition for salvation even though these truths are not contained in Holy Scripture nor can they be deduced from scripture alone. This position appears to me to be more probable than the other [that all saving truth is contained in scripture alone].[9]

On the other hand, Wessel Gansfort (1419–1489) of Grogingen adhered to a more rigid understanding of tradition. "Wessel Gansfort," writes Heiko Oberman, "did not reject the concept of tradition, as such, but rather a use of the tradition of the church as a second source of equal authority to the scriptures."[10] In fact he wrote: "I agree ... that regarding the rule of faith I ought to depend on the authority of the church with which - not in which - I believe." But more than once Gansfort expressed himself in a sense that was to become traditional, perhaps even conservative. Thus he remarks in a letter to Jacob Hoeck:

> I know very well that scripture alone is not a sufficient rule of faith. I know that some things which were not written were handed down by the Apostles and that all these teachings ought to be received into the rule of faith just like scripture.[11]

Gabriel Biel (ca. 1420–95), "the last of the scholastics," reviewed the problems arising from the relation of scripture to tradition. His handling of the central questions involved therein shows a certain degree of competence and conviction, but his contribution was not really original nor was it intended to be original. Still it is illuminating and represents what might properly be described as a classical position. Scripture contains revelation; so too, does tradition. Moreover, tradition contains revealed truths that are not to be found in scripture. It is, therefore, a supplementary source of divine revelation.[12]

Tradition, then, as a theological problem, was the province of specialists who dissected, analyzed, and examined it from various perspectives, but especially from the theological point of view. It was the scholastics of the late Middle Ages who formulated the problem of tradition which the sixteenth century finally inherited and which in one form or another has come down to our own day. Generally their formulation was concerned with scripture and tradition as the prime *loci* of revelation, the honor and respect due to them, and the degree of adherence which their authority commanded. It was typical of the method of the late medieval schoolmen to see in the religious monuments of the past arguments or evidence to establish the theological conclusions of the present. Their approach to scripture closely paralleled their approach to tradition.[13] Both were books of proof.

But at the same time the humanists were studying tradition with the hope that it might provide a foundation for a new understanding of Christian life. Erasmus (ca.1466–1536), for example, centered his research on the very sources of Christian tradition, the writings of the Fathers of the early church. He was seeking there a fresh concept of Christianity and a new kind of Christian life, unencumbered and unfettered by the trivial aspects of religion. He summed up his conception in the ancient expression *uera philosophia Christi*. Christianity would provide a distinctive way of life, structured on the wisdom of Christ and on his existential truth. It would plunder the treasures of the past, appropriating and incorporating them into the texture of life. The significance of the humanistic approach lay in the fact that it recognized the tradition of the church for exactly what it is, a source for understanding and appreciating the Christian experience in a full and meaningful way. For the humanist tradition imported above all else insight and inspiration; it was not simply a source of theological proof. That humanism never reached maturity is regrettable; its untimely disappearance from history is one of the unfortunate results of the Reformation.[14]

The origins and meanings of the Protestant Reformation are not obvious. It was a vast, complex religious movement involving manifold theological, social, political and economic factors. The extant source material is copious and diverse and shows no unified pattern of thought; discernment here runs the risk of deception. In a very real sense the problematic of the early phases of the Reformation concerned the meaning of Christian tradition. What up until then had been an academic and theological question suddenly became the burning issue of the day, the theme of pulpit and lectern, the gossip of town and gown. If the years 1517–1521 posed the question, "What is the church?" they also posed the questions, "What is scripture?" and "What is tradition?" Scripture and tradition were the earth-bound, man-made depositories of God's abiding word. They were like two bodies inhabited by one soul, or like two halves of one soul dwelling in the same body. The subsequent history of the great controversy shows that these questions coalesced into one: "What is Christianity?" which as a primordial mystery remains to this day without full answer.

In the history of the theology of tradition the early debates on the issue of indulgences opened a new chapter. Up to the first decades of the sixteenth century the problem of tradition was largely theological and, therefore, academic.

There was no reason for it to be otherwise. The concept of tradition as a religious reality had not been fully developed; the schools treated tradition as a theological subject. In pursuing its aims and objectives, scholasticism had its means and its method, and though it relied on tradition as a source, there was rarely question of establishing this tradition on the basis of sound history. And yet, in the decades before the appearance of Martin Luther (1483–1546) a new kind of scholarship was emerging which was restless with unsupported tradition and all that it implied.

As early as the days of the Franciscan exegete, Nicholas of Lyra (ca.1270–1340), it was clear that patristic thought would no longer be accepted on its face value and without challenge, that its authority was only as compelling as the reasons on which it rested, and that the days of the Fathers of the Church as inspired authors were now passing.[15] At the same time, the research of the humanists moved in the same direction as that of the exegetes. For example, Laurentio Valla's (ca.1406–1457) critical study of the Donation of Constantine successfully attacked what was then believed to be a prime tradition for establishing the temporal prerogatives of the papacy. It illustrates for us the incisive character of this new intellectual trend and shows how the development of textual criticism, biblical exegesis, and historical scholarship in the century before the reformation was threatening the authority of tradition as a theological locus.[16]

The first phase (1517–21) of the reformation controversy concerned Luther's protest against the abuse of the Christian religion and the response of the Roman church to that protest.[17] In view of his personal repugnance for the sale of indulgences Luther prepared a series of statements to enlighten Albrecht of Hohenzollern, the archbishop of the primatial see of Mainz, the archdiocese in which the indulgence scandal centered. Included in the packet of letters which he dispatched to Albrecht on October 31, 1517 were the following items: (1) a detailed description of the *de facto* situation; (2) a list of ninety-five theses to show the uncertainty of the theology of indulgences: and (3) a theological treatise on the meaning of indulgences. As a university professor Luther was well within his rights in pointing out a scandal in the church's ministry, in condemning it, and appealing to competent authority against it. Apart from certain frivolous and sarcastic theses, the list as a whole adumbrates Luther's subsequent comprehension of the church as an institution "within" which but not "through" which there is salvation. The emphasis here falls on the exteriority rather than on the interiority of the church, on the church as occasion, but not as means, of salvation.[18]

The appeal of Luther to Archbishop Albrecht terminated in his denunciation to Pope Leo X. This was the irony of history. Instead of Albrecht having to justify his bad theology to Luther, it was Luther who was ordered to explain his bad conduct to Leo. This took the form of a private meeting in October of 1518 with the renowned Cardinal Cajetan, the pope's legate at the imperial diet of Augsburg. A papal brief had cited Luther before him. The discussion was to be Luther's only personal confrontation with a member of the Roman Curia in the course of his career. It was arranged so that he might be induced to recant his doctrinal stance and correct his public deportment. Above all the meeting was to be irenic. The cardinal was explicitly instructed by the pope not to debate or to dispute with Luther, not to contend nor to be contentious, but merely to explain the doctrinal position of the Holy See and the grave consequences of not conforming to it, and finally to secure Luther's recantation and his cooperation for the future. A modus agendi was carefully worked out to provide for every legal contingency in handling the case.[19]

Apart from other considerations cultural, intellectual,

and political, the confrontation of Luther with Cajetan on October 12, 13, 14 represents an instance of history serving as a symbol of a higher truth, for here two very different and distinct streams of thought run counter to one another, mingle and then explode with force. In Cajetan we hear the voice of Thomas; in Luther, the voice of Augustine. The Dominican is objective and ecclesial; the Augustinian, subjective and personal. Cajetan was a metaphysician; Luther, an exegete. Both were essentially conservative, each in his own way, for both wished to preserve a tradition, the Christian tradition, even though they viewed it differently. The historical development of the colloquy at Augsburg shows the inability of these two minds and personalities to meet, to understand one another and to be sympathetic of their basic differences.

To Cajetan it was unthinkable that Christian theology could subsist and thrive without the support of tradition (of that venerable apostolic tradition whose roots went back to Jesus Christ himself). After all, this was fundamental to theology whose primary concern was to discover and express the sense of divine revelation. For Luther, who had begun to formulate his theological method even before the autumn of 1518, theology rests on and is fed by one source—scripture and scripture alone. From it faith derives, and what does not derive from it is unworthy of Christian faith. It is not surprising that the last session between Cajetan and Luther terminated in tension, frustration, shouting, and, finally, alienation.[20]

The second stage in the development of Luther's theological method emerged in the Leipzig Debate in July 1519. In the few months which had elapsed since the Colloquy at Augsburg, the center of interest shifted from the meaning and efficacy of indulgences to church order and structure, concretely to the magisterial competence of pope and council. The central question was posed this way: "Does the church derive such authority from Jesus Christ that through its chief representatives, the pope and the council, it teaches faith and morals without error?" Whereas the confrontation at Augsburg had been private, the debate at Leipzig was public. The former was a dialogue; the latter, a disputation. The issue at Augsburg was subsisiary; at Leipzig, it was pivotal. It was not merely a question of the pope as primate in the church, as custodian of law and order in the community, as the spiritual overseer of Christendom, and as the one and only successor of St. Peter. The central question was epistomological: "How does the church become aware of the truth which it believes and teaches?" That is an important question, going in fact to the heart of the Christian faith and its living tradition.

Luther's opponent at Leipzig was the renowned Dr. Johannes Eck (1486–1543), professor at the university of Ingolstadt. He was eloquent, relentless, perhaps even ruthless; he was well informed, retentive, and eager to dispute with Luther whom he had already taken to task in writing. He was a theologian of some originality, an author whose work was noticed. He was not insignificant, and he was a debater almost by nature. Eck was "galling to Luther because he was an old friend, not a mendicant but a humanist, not a perfidious Italian but a German, and not the least because he was formidable."[21] He was more than a match for Luther at Leipzig, and his powerful attack seriously hurt the reformer's self-esteem and damaged his image. For this "outrage" Eck was never forgiven by Luther, by those who came after him, or by generations of Protestant historians. Perhaps had he been dim-witted and incapable of articulating and maintaining his theological position he would have been pardoned as graciously as the unfortunate Tetzel had been. But Eck had a mind of his own and knew how to express it. It was his mind at Leipzig to establish and defend Catholic truth by discrediting the theological method of

Luther. The prospect of hurt feelings neither persuaded nor discouraged him, nor was he even slightly concerned about the unfriendliness and hostility of the Wittenbergers who surrounded him on all sides at Leipzig.

The Leipzig Debate went without decision. The theological issues were too delicate and sensitive to allow the official judges to evaluate the merits of the disputants. Besides, the matter of victory or defeat was not as important as the significant shift in theological method and doctrinal perspective that the debate witnessed on the part of Luther. The drift towards scriptural autonomy was slow, direct, and well-defined. By and in itself scripture was to be regarded as the decisive norm in solving both theological and religious problems. As the ultimate authority, the incontestable criterion, and the absolute rule of faith, it was above pope and council, above church and tradition. All must be based on scripture and on scripture alone. All that is in scripture must be believed, and all that must be believed is in scripture. All rests on scripture; scripture rests on God. From him alone it derives its dignity and its authority, its majesty and its glory. This concept of faith and word finds its classical formulation in the expression—*scriptura sola*.

The proposition around which the Leipzig Debate raged most passionately concerned the origins of the superiority of the church of Rome over and above all others. It read thus:

> The very feeble decrees of the Roman pontiffs which have appeared in the last four hundred years prove that the Roman church is superior to all others. Against them stand the history of eleven hundred years, the text of divine scripture, and the decree of the Council of Nicaea, the most sacred of all councils.[22]

It was in the debate on this proposition that the different theological methods represented by Eck and Luther clashed most fiercely and incisively. The assertion that the church of Rome was superior to all others in Christendom rested on the witness of tradition but not on the text of Holy Scripture. It was presumed to be the conclusion of the accumulated witness of history, but for Luther no proof rooted solely in tradition was acceptable; he demanded the ultimate, the evidence of the sacred text.

There is a paradox here. If Eck's position on the superiority of the Church of Rome could not be verified from the very words of scripture neither could Luther's principle, *scriptura sola*. Nowhere does scripture teach that it is the exclusive source of faith, the unique deposit of revelation and the inspired Word of God. Nowhere does scripture explicitly teach the principle, *scriptura sola*. In the first quarter of the sixteenth century the Catholic epistomological problem was acute. Tradition, as it descended from the Middle Ages was contaminated; in consequence it posed difficult problems. Long, reckless confrontation with history had damaged it, and rendered its witness uncertain. It needed to be justified, validated, and purified; it was, therefore, to be used with care and prudence. It is understandable that Luther was restless with tradition; that he finally repudiated it is unfortunate, but it was not easy for him to get along without it. His position was far more precarious than he realized. If he recognized the inadequacy of tradition apart from scripture, he did not perceive the insufficiency of scripture apart from tradition. If Eck could not perfectly derive his position from the text of scripture, neither could Luther derive his, and that is ironic above all else.

Luther's conception of the uniqueness of scripture as an authority made all other *primordia* superfluous - pope, council, and especially tradition. Christianity became a religion of the book, read not by the church as its book (which it had been historically) but by the individual as his book (which it had never been before). Thus, at Leipzig Luther spoke of the primacy of scripture this way:

> A simple layman armed with scripture is to be believed above a pope or a council without it. As for the pope's decretal on indulgences I say that neither the church nor the pope can establish articles of faith. These must come from scripture. For the sake of scripture we should reject pope and council.[23]

This was an understanding of the church and its magisterial role so different from the church of tradition that it inspired the pointed questions: "Luther, are you alone clever? Are you alone right, Luther, and are all others wrong?" Luther's conception of the self-sufficiency of scripture was greatly overdrawn. It was expressed in brave, new, rhetorical terms, but it was defenseless and vulnerable without the comfort and the support of authority.

The Catholics took sharp issue with Luther's repudiation of tradition; on the other hand, the Anabaptists were enraged with his exaltation of scripture. They contended that the Spirit, who was above the bible, resided with them. "Bible, babble, bubble!" they said to Luther. "Scripture is convincing to the convinced." And later at the Colloquy of Marburg (1529) with Ulrich Zwingli (1484–1531) Luther himself demonstrated the inherent weakness of the principle *scriptura sola*. When the Swiss reformer refused to accept the traditional and conservative sense of the text, *hoc est corpus meum,* Luther refused to extend to him and to "the ranting spirits" the right hand of fellowship. For the church *scriptura sola* was a declarative rather than a constitutive principle; it was acceptable and accepted wherever there was a consensus on the fundamentals of faith.

Luther's insight into the relation of scripture and tradition was not original. It finds its point of departure in one well-defined stream of late medieval theology according to which scripture and tradition are so coextensive that the latter is perfectly contained in the former. The formula, *scriptura sola,* where *sola* cancels *traditio,* is another way of saying the same thing, that tradition as a shadow of scripture lacks substance apart from it. At the Diet of Worms (April of 1521), when Luther was questioned about the different books attributed to him: ". . . Do you or do you not repudiate your books and the errors which they contain?" he replied:

> Since then your serene majesty and your lordships seek a simple answer, I will give it in this manner, neither horned nor toothed: Unless I am convinced by the testimony of the scriptures or by clear reason (for I do not trust either in the pope or in councils alone, since it is well-known that they have often erred and contradicted themselves), I am bound by the scriptures I have quoted and my conscience is captive to the Word of God. I cannot and I will not retract anything, since it is neither safe nor right to go against my conscience.[24]

For Luther it was as simple as that. He would be convinced by scripture and plain reason or he would not be convinced at all. The authority of popes and councils was repudiated because it could be justified only on the evidence of tradition, and tradition could not be justified on the evidence of scripture. This, therefore, was Luther's "simple answer" to the diet.

Throughout the earliest stage of the Lutheran controversy the debate invariably involved theological method, and implicitly raised questions such as: "What is dogma?" "How is it established?" "Why is it privileged?" Luther's stress on the unique role of scripture in justifying and defending dogma was not an innovation. The supreme authority of scripture in matters of faith and morals had been universally recognized and honored long before his day. No one in the Middle Ages believed that dogma was an arbitrary and capricious statement formulated without need of adverting to the witness of Holy Scripture. The new element, therefore, was not Luther's insistence on the preponderance of scripture; it was rather his contention that scripture by itself alone was the one and only norm for determining all truth worthy of Christian faith. In this he differed greatly from his predecessors who held that scripture was indeed decisive but only to the extent that it was read and interpreted by the church as its book.

In the great theological debate of the sixteenth century the Catholics were at a disadvantage. That well may have been their own fault in accepting *scriptura sola* as a methodological principle, even though only for the sake of discussion with their adversaries. Scripture would not yield the proof that the reformers demanded, and the proof that tradition yielded the reformers would not accept. It was clear that if the dialogue was to be ongoing and meaningful, the concept of tradition would have to be shaped to allow it to play a broader and more comprehensive role. The tendency, therefore, was to develop tradition beside scripture as a source of divine revelation and as a source of theological proof.

The pristine sense of tradition seems to have been buried under the debris of history.[25] This is dramatically illustrated in certain attitudes discernible in the discussions preparatory to the fourth session (April 8, 1546) of the Council of Trent and to the promulgation of its decree on revelation. The prehistory of this session is worth recounting, for it exemplifies how misunderstood the concept of tradition had become by the middle of the sixteenth century. The attempts made by different theologians at the council to catalogue apostolic (and other) traditions known to and accepted by the church show a surprising lack of acquaintance with the vast dimensions of the problem.[26] These catalogues also reveal how poorly the differences in character of the truths which constitute tradition were discerned. We see here no conscious effort to differentiate levels and moments, e.g.: dogmatic, disciplinary, apostolic, and ecclesiastical; and this despite the insistence of the Jesuit theologian Claude LeJay (ca. 1500–52) that the different elements of Christian tradition must be carefully evaluated and distinguished.[27]

But the preparation of the council's decree on scripture and tradition created a series of difficulties that give valuable insight into the state of the question at that time. One problem turned on the council's formula that revelation is simply divided between (*partim . . . partim*) scripture and tradition as two, separate, independent fonts which complement one another.[28] This formulation was finally set aside by the council. Verbally it was too assertive; conceptually it was too incisive. Another problem turned on the phrase, *pari pietatis affectu ac reverentia.* Here the council wanted to express the veneration with which it (and, therefore, the church) should accept scripture and tradition. According to its decree "equal love and reverance" are to be paid to both of them.[29] This way of speaking seemed to equate the two by assigning equal honor and reverence to them as fonts of God's revelation. The phrase, therefore, engendered suspicion. It was offensive; it degraded the majesty and authority of the divinely inspired word; and it neglected the consideration that scripture is from God; tradition from man. To equate the two is contrary to the *sensus Christianus;* worse still, it is blasphemy.

How this conception of the problem affected the fathers of the council appears vividly in the great altercation—the *magnus tumultus* as Seripando described it—that broke out in the general congregation on April 5th. Here Bishop Nacchianti of Chioggia voiced indignation that the council's teaching was moving towards equating scripture and tradition. His words were well calculated to stir feelings deeply and to make tempers rise sharply. "It is ungodly (*impium*)," he shouted, "to put scripture and tradition on the same level!" When Francisco de Navarra, the bishop of Badajoz, asked: "Are we ungodly people?" he was answered in harsh, even angry words: "Yes, I repeat it! How can I accept the practice of praying eastward with the same reverence as St. John's gospel?"[30]

This exchange allows us to see how even the best minds of that time had a distorted concept of Christian tradition. The character of the truths which were believed to be part of tradition was not defined. Thus all kinds of truths came to be included in its deposit, and in the course of time these different truths came to enjoy an equality of dignity that was disproportionate. In terms of this meaning of tradition, the resentment of Bishop Nacchianti is understandable, for he could not see how the authority of God's word contained in the inspired scriptures could be properly equated to the various odds and ends preserved in what was then believed to be Christian tradition.

The council finally published its decree on scripture and tradition. It read in part:

[The council] also clearly perceives that the truth and the teaching [of Jesus Christ] are contained in written books and in unwritten traditions, which were received by the Apostles from the mouth of Christ himself, or from the Apostles themselves to whom the Holy Spirit dictated them. [This teaching] has come down to us, transmitted as if from hand to hand. Following, then, the example of the orthodox Fathers, [the council] receives and venerates with equal piety and reverence all the books of the Old as well as of the New Testament, since the one God is the author of both, also the traditions . . . as having been dictated either orally by Christ or by the Holy Spirit, and preserved in the Catholic Church in unbroken succession.[31]

Perhaps this decree was the theologian's ideal. It said enough about tradition to secure a place for it in theology, to establish it as a font of revelation, to honor it as the memory of the church. But it did not remove all obscurities. The problems which tradition has created in the course of time are perennial; doubtlessly they will abide with us as long as there are theologians preoccupied with understanding the mystery of the church as she fulfills her magisterial role in the context of history and on behalf of mankind.

Notes

1. Cf. the original title of his book, *Herfsttijd der Middeleeuwen* (Haarlem, 1919), which unfortunately is translated *The Waning of the Middle Ages* (London, 1924).
2. Cf. Heiko Oberman in *Forerunners of the Reformation* (New York, 1966) pp. 9ff., who seems to think that the moral integrity of pre-Reformation society can be salvaged from its negative reputation. Even the best of good will and the most broadminded of observers are powerless to give a favorable interpretation of the situation.
3. Cf. Gerhard Ladner, "Homo Viator: Mediaeval Ideas on Alienation and Order," *Speculum* 42 (1967) p. 253: "Around 1330 . . . the Middle Ages had already been gripped by the first spasms of that dreadful mass alienation which expressed itself in the interrelated phenomena of witch cult and witch hunt."
4. Cf. Charles de Tolnay, *Hieronymus Bosch* (Baden-Baden, 1966) pl. 60. Beneath the figure of Christ who surveys the seven principal sins and sinners are inscribed the words: "Cave! Cave! Dominus videt."
5. Cf. Joseph Jungmann, "Der Stand des liturgischen Lebens am Vorabend der Reformation," *Liturgisches Erbe und pastorale Gegenwart* (Innsbruck, 1960) pp. 87 ff.

6. R. E. McNally, "Medieval Exegesis," *Theological Studies* 22 (1961) pp. 447–48.

7. Ludolphus de Saxonia, *Vita Iesu Christi, Prooemium* 11, ed. L. M. Rigollot, 1 (Paris, 1878) p. 7. The tendency revealed here is older than Ludolph's work. It is found, for example, in the highly influential *Meditationes de vita Christi* of Pseudo-Bonaventure (13th-14th century Franciscan circle), which most certainly was known to Ludolph. Cf. Jean Leclercq, F. Vandenbroucke, and Louis Bouyer, *La spiritualité du Moyen-Age* 2 (Paris, 1961) pp. 380–81.

8. Cf. Heiko Oberman, *The Harvest of Medieval Theology* (Cambridge, Mass., 1963) pp. 365 ff.

9. Oberman, *Forerunners*, p. 72.

10. *Ibid.*, p. 65.

11. *Ibid.*, p. 105.

12. Cf. Oberman, *Harvest*, pp. 393 ff.

13. The approach of scholastics and humanists to scripture and tradition as sources differed greatly. The former excessively stressed their probative value and the need for arguments of theology to be structured on their evidence. Cf. R. E. McNally, *The Unreformed Church* (New York, 1965) pp. 88 ff., and R. Guelluy, "L'evolution des methodes théologiques à Louvain d'Erasme à Jansenius," *Revue d'histoire ecclesiastique* 37 (1941) pp. 31–144.

14. Cf. A. Rabil, *Erasmus and the New Testament: The Mind of a Christian Humanist* (San Antonio, 1972) pp. 103 ff.; and Lewis W. Spitz, *The Religious Renaissance of the German Humanists* (Cambridge, Mass., 1963) pp. 227 ff. I have, however, certain reservations about Spitz' comprehension of Erasmus' Catholicism.

15. Ceslaus Spicq, *Esquisse d'une histoire de l'exégèse latine au Moyen-Age* (Paris, 1944) pp. 339–40.

16. Cf. Robert Herndon Fife, *The Revolt of Martin Luther* (New York, 1957) pp. 472 ff. Though Valla's conclusions were mainly concerned with the origins of the temporal power of the papacy, they had repercussions for the papal office itself and its spiritual prerogatives.

17. Cf. Luther's letter of October 31, 1517, to Albrecht of

Hohenzollern in *The Reformation,* ed. Hans J. Hillerbrand (New York, 1964) pp. 49–51.

18. Cf. R. E. McNally, "The Ninety-Five Theses of Martin Luther: 1517–1967," *Theological Studies* 28 (1967) pp. 461 ff.

19. Cf. R. E. McNally, "The Roman Process of Martin Luther: A Failure in Subsidiarity," in *The Once and Future Church,* ed. J. A. Coriden (New York, 1971) pp. 111–28.

20. *The Proceedings at Augsburg,* trans. Harold Grimm, *Luther's Works* 31 (Philadelphia, 1957) pp. 275–77.

21. Roland H. Bainton, *Here I Stand: A Life of Martin Luther* (New York, 1950) p. 82. "Eck was the Goliath of the Philistines."

22. *The Leipzig Debate,* trans. Harold Grimm, *Luther's Works* 31 (Philadelphia, 1957) p. 318.

23. Bainton, *op. cit.,* p. 90.

24. *Luther at the Diet of Worms,* trans. R. A. Hornsby, *Luther's Works* 32 (Philadelphia, 1958) p. 112.

25. By way of exception the thinking of the Servite General Agostino Bonuccio on tradition was sufficiently ancient and conservative as to appear modern and liberal: "Tradition is essentially an authoritative interpretation of Holy Writ, not its complement," Hubert Jedin, *A History of the Council of Trent* 2 (Saint Louis, 1961) p. 75. Girolamo Seripando defined tradition as "the holy and salutary ordinances (*constitutiones*) of the apostles and the holy fathers which have always been in the church," Hubert Jedin, *Papal Legate at the Council of Trent* (London, 1947) p. 277.

26. Jedin, *History,* 2, 62–63. The layman Count Lodovico Nogarola submitted to the council a list of no less than thirty-four apostolic traditions. The papal legate, Cardinal Cervini, who was generally opposed to the enumeration of individual traditions, had learned the futility of this exercise from personal experience.

27. *Ibid.,* 2, 62. The treatise *De traditionibus (Concilium Tridentinum* 12, 522 ff.) may be the work of LeJay, who distinguished two kinds of traditions: dogmatic, concerned with faith, and nondogmatic, concerned with nonsubstantive truth; the former of divine origin, the latter of human origin.

28. Jedin, *History* 2, 75. Jedin's words here are worthy of note:

"There can be no doubt that though the majority of the theologians of Trent may not have approved the formula *partim-partim*, they approved the thing itself, that is, the statement that dogmatic tradition was a channel of revelation which supplemented the scriptures."

29. Cf. *ibid.*, 2, 74 ff., 82 ff. Actually the council only intended by the formula *pari pietatis affectu ac reverentia* to stress the fact that reverence is due to God's revealed word in itself (*id quod*) rather than in its modality (*modus quo*). God's word is revered not only because it is inspired, but simply because it is God's word.

30. *Ibid.*, 2, 86–87.

31. Sessio IV (8 April 1546): Decretum primum: recipiuntur libri sacri et traditiones apostolorum, in *Conciliorum Oecumenicorum Decreta*, ed. J. Alberigo et al. (Freiburg-im-Breisgau, 1962) p. 639.

CHAPTER FIVE

Tradition In Theology: A Problematic Approach

George H. Tavard

In the sixteenth century, the great divisions of the Protestant Reformation were occasioned, among other deep reasons, by divergences of views on the value of the Christian past, in the postapostolic period, as a permanent norm of the faith. Certainly this was neither the primary nor the first question for Martin Luther: the problem of justification was the *articulus stantis aut cadentis ecclesiae*. But Luther's Catholic adversaries refuted him, not on the ground of redemption and salvation, but on that of the tradition as a norm of faith. To reject the normative aspect of the tradition and to appeal to scripture alone became a polemical, rather than a dogmatic, necessity of the Reformation.

That this was a polemical rather than a dogmatic necessity tallies with the fact that the divisions between Catholics and Protestants on the nature of the tradition have now been bypassed by the evolution of the theological problematic. Except in popular presentations of the faith, the sharp oppositions on the structure of salvation and on the nature of the Christian life which emerged in the sixteenth century, are nowhere to be found today. On the contrary, a unanimous agreement has been reached, in theology if not

84

in popular practice, on the absolute necessity of grace for salvation. Theologians of all sides recognize that the classical Catholic vocabulary on the merits of the works of faith presupposes the prevenient grace of God: by rewarding the merits of each, God crowns the merits of Christ who lives and acts in the hearts of the faithful. The book of Hans Küng on justification at the Council of Trent and for Karl Barth, in which the convergence of doctrine was emphasized, raised no basic objections when it appeared in 1957. Agreement on justification is now a fact. The progressive abandonment by Catholic authors of the vocabulary of merit and reward constitutes the other side of this coin.

One may therefore wonder if differences between Catholics and Protestants on the other chief problem of the Reformation—the polemical position on scripture alone—are still justified. Having arisen in the sixteenth century out of the debates over justification, the Reformers' argumentation against tradition in favor of *scriptura sola* has now lost most of its edge. Furthermore, several additional convergences should be noted.

The rapid evolution of exegetical methods and of hermeneutics is now practically the same in Catholic and Protestant theology. On each side, the doctrinal tradition no longer plays its former role. When exegetes and theologians were looking for the spiritual senses of the bible they needed sources in the tradition, for fear the spiritual senses they would discover and apply were their own arbitrary creations. Today's concern is more for a historical knowledge, in depth, of the biblical message. The history of the church and of theology in postapostolic times cannot be the source of such a knowledge. As a result, the historical dimension of religious thought which we call tradition loses some of its former status.

Moreover, contemporary theological systematization, at

its most dynamic and creative, does not give historical research the privileged place it enjoyed in Catholic theology between the two world wars and up to Vatican Council II. Having prepared and, if we must say so, made the Council of the Vatican, historical theology, grounded in a more thorough knowledge of the Fathers than used to be the case in Western Christianity, is now receding into the background. Admittedly, the best known theologians of the postconciliar era can still work historically, as Karl Rahner or Hans Küng have done. Yet they are not particularly influential as historians. Their importance comes from their attempt to work out a new theological methodology. Rahner has opted for a phenomenological method which seems to me of particularly hazardous use by less gifted thinkers than Rahner. Küng uses a complex combination of phenomenological reflection and existential hermeneutics. In these conditions, the tradition no longer sits at the central place it was given by scholastic theology, by recent neoscholastic theology, and by the positive or historical theology of our century. The growing interest in theological methodology, as instanced by Bernard Lonergan's *Method in Theology,* indicates indeed that theology is undergoing a mutation that touches directly on its methods. This affects, in particular, the nature and task of the appeal to tradition.

Before going further in our reflection, a few words should be said about tradition at the stages of Counter-Reformation scholasticism and positive theology.

I

At the time of speculative theology, tradition was interpreted as the totality of the *sensus ecclesiae,* as found in the theological documents and in the doctrinal and canonical norms inherited from the past. In his polemics against

Catholics like Richard Simon, Fénelon, Charlas, and against Protestants, Bossuet appealed to the "sense of the church" which emerged, in his opinion, from the documents, and which his adversaries, according to him, neglected or misunderstood. But it is self-evident that, in the process by which documents are interpreted, the documents themselves are not the most important element. Much more important will be the principles according to which the texts will be interpreted. Thus, tradition as a norm of faith or of theology does not exist in itself. Tradition acquires the status of a norm when a theologian proceeds to its reconstruction, when he discovers its constitutive elements and sketches in retrospect the main lines of its direction. In the perspective of speculative theology, tradition is never the voice of the past as such. Rather, the voice of the past becomes tradition through the mediation of theological reconstruction, when theologians, canonists, bishops, popes, councils, formulate it and, in order to formulate it, imagine it, re-create it.

In this reconstruction, history and historical research play an important role. They provide the material—one could say the raw material—in which the theologian will try to find the missing documents without which his *sensus ecclesiae* could not identify with any probability the *sensus* of the generality of the church in the period he is considering. Because the church does not live only in the present but has accumulated the memory of a past whose spiritual substance still enriches it, history belongs to the fabric of its structure and to the horizon of its existence. But if history provides the constitutive elements of tradition, tradition itself is born and comes to life in the perceptive insights of theologians and their enlightened interpretations of the past.

In this perspective, one should correct a standard assumption of the textbooks and of some recent studies concerning tradition. The distinction between a documentary tradition and a living tradition opposed, in the nineteenth century, the school of Rome and the school of Tübingen. The school of Tübingen, with Sebastian Drey and Johann Adam Möhler, would have restored the notion of a living tradition, identified with the self-awareness of the church at any period of its history; large traces of this view may be found in the Constitution *Dei Verbum* of Vatican II. The school of Rome, dominated by professors in the Roman universities, such as Perrone and Franzelin, would have perpetuated and amplified a documentary conception of tradition as the written documentation inherited from the past. With Perrone, this conception raised objections to Newman's theory of the development of Christian doctrine, which of course implied a view of tradition closer to that of the school of Tübingen.[1]

Indeed, the accents of these two theological orientations are different, even divergent. Yet when they studied the documents of the past in order to extract the tradition from them, the theologians of Rome were exactly in the same position as those of Tübingen. They acted as sounding boards of the voice of the past so that this voice could acquire meaning and resonance in their time. The documents speak only to the extent that they are read and interpreted in the ongoing life of the interpreting community. There is accordingly, in my judgment, a certain exaggeration and oversimplification in Yves Congar's analysis of the Counter Reformation. In his important study, *Tradition and Traditions,* Congar sees the post-Tridentine theology of tradition as bringing about a major turning point in the history of the matter when it opted for a documentary approach to the past.[2] Two remarks should be made. In the first place, there cannot be a tradition without a reference to the past and therefore without some sort of written or other documentation about the past. In the second place, such documentation reaches the status, the form and the scope of tradition only when it has passed through the catalyst constituted by the reflexive mind of theologians. Documentary or not, the tradition of the past exists only in the present. On this point, Bossuet in his many polemics, Pius IX against rationalism, Pius X against modernism, and all the champions of the old tradition against the Reformers were in exactly the same situation as Saint Augustine in the fifth century, Hincmar of Rheims in the ninth, or Saint Thomas Aquinas in the thirteenth: starting from the documents which they knew, they had to reinterpret the past by reconstructing it in the light of the present and in anticipation of the future as they imagined it.

By the same token, Heiko Oberman's typology, which ascribes three successive and mutually incompatible forms to the dominant theology of tradition in Catholicism, is fallacious.[3] Oberman equates Tradition I with the straightforward preaching of the kerygma; Tradition II with an extrabiblical source of doctrines; Tradition III with the living teaching *magisterium* in the church. The first conception would have flourished in the early church; the second would have grown in the Middle Ages, and the Council of Trent would have canonized it; the third would have developed through the Counter Reformation and been endorsed by Vatican I. The above remarks should be repeated here. Even though special accents and orientations may characterize the three periods which are somewhat artificially distinguished by Oberman, the catalyst by which the past becomes relevant to the present remains exactly the same in all cases. The mind of the preacher is always the medium of the kerygma; the mind of the theologian always interprets the scriptural or other sources of doctrine; the mind of the hierarchy, expressed in a council or, more haphazardly, outside of a council, formulates and applies the conclusions gathered by reflection on the revealed data. In all these cases, the key to the tradition is always the living and lived self-consciousness of the thinking members of the church.

II

In regard to historical or positive theology, tradition appears in a rather different light. Historical theology, as distinct both from history and from speculative or systematic theology, developed in the seventeenth century in France with the remarkable works of Petau and Thomassin.[4] Whereas these authors composed huge syntheses which were analogous in scope, although dissimilar in method, with the speculative *summae,* recent historical theologians, such as Henri de Lubac or Jean Daniélou, have been more modest in their ambitions but more thorough in their analyses and more promising in their conclusions. Positive theology has come into its own in our century by focusing on specific doctrines. In this method of approach to theological questions tradition has become the very soul of theology. The contemporary theological vision, which emerges for instance from the works of de Lubac,[5] derives from a historical investigation into the movement of tradition on the point under study. The purpose is not to gather historical documentation: this is a preliminary requirement which is theological in purpose but not in method. The theologian's purpose is to read the documents, to interpret the events, to understand the movement of history in the evolving theological thought of the church, so that each event is explained by all the others. In this sort of comparative reading, illustrations are sought both in the synchrony of each period and, since the time limits of historical periods are little more than views of the mind which need to be constantly corrected by attention to the flow of events, in the diachrony of each movement of thought. A sort of collective meaning of documents and events is thus elicited from the facts as they are known. This collective meaning yields the *sensus ecclesiae,* the mind of the church, the growing self-awareness of the Christian community, the guidance of the Spirit toward the full truth of Christ's revelation. Thus the church is seen bringing to the surface the doctrinal and vital orientations of its spiritual depths.

This kind of theology, which I have myself practiced in some of my writings,[6] is itself a movement of discovery within the faith. It is also, although in a different way from that of speculative thought, *fides quaerens intellectum.* The testimony of a past theologian—be this a Father of the Church, a schoolman or a more recent author—is not studied for its own sake, for theology is not historical erudition, whatever need one may have of such erudition; it is looked into for the sake of what can be unveiled of the self-awareness of the corporate mind of the church.

As a matter of fact, a direct tie seems to bind together positive theology and a Catholic or Catholicizing conception of the church as body of Christ. Positive theology has been practiced chiefly by Catholics and by Anglicans. Neither Lutherans nor Calvinists have, by and large, favored such a methodology. Being primarily concerned with the problem of man as sinner and saved, Lutheran dogmatics did not orient theological research toward the historical discovery of the *sensus ecclesiae,* of the self-awareness of the church conceived as a socio-mystical body. Primarily concerned with the authenticity of biblical faith, Calvinism could not of itself encourage searching for the church's self-awareness outside of the scriptures and of a few commentaries on the scriptures. On the contrary, the very horizon of the Catholic institution favored a historical investigation which would go beyond history and reach a real intellection of the faith.

Yet a catalyst is at work in the gathering together of

historical evidence and in the study of the doctrinal and theological documents of the past. No theological conclusion would emerge from a historical investigation without a mediation. It is precisely the personal reflection of the enquirer which provides the necessary and sufficient element through which a return to the past becomes a *resourcement,* enabling him to understand the thrust of faith and the teachings of the church in the present day. The past comes to life as tradition through the action of a contemporary living reflection which cannot avoid being contextual and conditioned by its time. Tradition exists only as a contemporary interpretation of the past in the light of the expected future.

III

We thus reach an important conclusion. Whether we consider tradition in the perspective of its use in the speculative or scholastic theology or in a historical theology, the tradition is never seen as a mere reference to the past. The documents which unveil the past to us become tradition only to the extent that they are selected, assessed and interpreted here and now. In other words, there is no theological tradition without a reference to the present and to the signs of the times which characterize the contemporary period. In the final analysis, tradition is built up for us and by us out of the past under the felt influence of the Spirit in today's church.

Indeed, one could analyze tradition from the standpoint of memory and define it as the church's memory. As such, it includes primarily the remembrance of the great acts of God in Jesus Christ and even, before that, of the interventions of God in the life of his people from Abraham to John the Baptist. It includes also the high moments of the successive existence of the church through ages. There are theologians of the Counter Reformation who compared this to the memory of a people or a nation, by which customs, principles, tales, techniques, are preserved and transmitted. Thus, John Sergeant distinguished between the natural, immediate effect of tradition—human faith in the reliability of the church's memory—and the supernatural, remote, effect, namely, true saving faith:

> The immediate effect of our tradition is human faith; the remote effect is to give us knowledge of a doctrine of faith which is divine, not proved to be such by tradition, but acknowledged to be so by our mutual concession. . . . Human faith is the way or means to know divine faith.[7]

A similar understanding of tradition as the human race's memory was at the heart of the school of Traditionalism which flourished in Europe during the nineteenth century and had no little influence on the First Vatican Council, even though the Council rejected its more extreme view of the nature of our knowledge of God as stemming from tradition rather than each person's perception of causality in the created universe.

More recently, tradition as memory has been studied with deeper insight into the specifically Christian structure of the memory of the Lord in the memorial that the Lord left us. The church is the eucharistic community. It remembers the death and the resurrection of the Lord. This *anamnesis,* or memorial in the full sense of the term, implies rather more than what is meant by remembrance. Admittedly, one can give a strong sense to remembering. As Fernand Guimet describes it,[8] the act of remembering implies that something in the human psyche, namely, memory, escapes the deleterious conditions of time. To remember the past in the present, which is the proper function of memory, is to bring forth, to elicit, an aspect of past events under which these are not over and done with, but rather are assumed in an eternal instant. In a way, memory participates of eternity, bringing men and women who remember to the level, in a fleeting moment, of God's eternal present. Yet the church's memory implies something more concrete. For at the heart of the church's memory of Jesus is the memorial, the eucharist, Christ made present by the power of the spirit during the commemorative meal of his death and resurrection. Through the liturgical memorial the faithful share in the apostolic experience of Christ. Thus the eucharist is at the origin and at the center of tradition, both in the passive sense of what is transmitted (the eucharist as Christ given for the many) and in the active sense of the act of transmission (the eucharist as the central action of Christian initiation, preaching and teaching). Likewise, all Christian tradition is eucharistic, because to hand on the memory-memorial of the *acta et passa Christi* implies giving thanks to the Father for the philanthropy which bestowed on us the gift of his Son.

Yet one may go further. For there is no tradition without a reference to the future. It is in the light of the expected future that we interpret the past into the tradition. I explained this at length at the end of my study of tradition in the seventeenth century.[9] To state it briefly, it seems that human life and thought are always lived and thought in the light of a project, of an expectation, of an anticipation concerning the shape of the future. Human beings did not wait for the invention of futurology to make hypotheses about their future. Maurice Blondel in particular analyzed the nature of human action insofar as it always unveils, albeit succinctly and briefly, the shape of a project.[10] To act is to do something that will necessarily, for good or for bad, shape the future. Our acts are therefore dependent on an anticipation of what the future ought to be if it is to meet our emotional desires, to satisfy our intellectual convictions, to allow our ambitions to be fulfilled.

The acts by which the church, or a sizable and influential proportion of its members, sorts out the facts of the past, seeing some as genuine elements of the continuing tradition, branding others as aberrant events without inherent value, yet useful by the contrast they present with the tradition, are themselves influenced by the church's anticipation of its future. They depend on an eschatology in regard to the posthistorical transformation of the universe, and on a hope concerning the continuing mission of the church in the world. The recent theologies of hope have done little more than focus attention, with excessive exclusiveness, on a permanent and unavoidable aspect of the Christian tradition. The past becomes tradition insofar as it is shaped by the anticipated future.

This could be shown also by analysis of tradition as memory. For memory, in the mystical tradition,[11] is the faculty of hope. It is the art of forgetting, of giving up impediments, of placing between us and the world the cloud of unknowing that will enable us to proceed unhampered into the deeper Cloud of Unknowing which is the experience of the living God. We remember insofar as we forget what is not worth remembering. Thus we are able to turn to the future with hope. Likewise, it is in view of the eternal gospel that the Church remembers the gospel in its tradition. The promises are cherished because they tend to a fulfillment.

In this also theological tradition is eucharistic. The eucharist implies a prospective tension toward the coming fullness of the epiphany, when the evidence of the Lord's resurrection will be totally unfolded by his return as the Consummator of Creation and the Last Judge. But Christian eschatology is one. The eschatological dimension of tradition and that of the eucharist are not to be connumerated. Rather, they constitute two aspects of a basic Christian attitude, the desire for the fullness of life in the kingdom. This fullness is experienced in the eucharist by anticipation.

The wish for it is the driving force in the church's mission and in the nisus of tradition toward the future.[12]

Such a perspective brings a complementary point into light. The tradition is never finalized. It evolves as it is apprehended by successive generations whose views of the Christian future cannot be entirely isomorphic, and whose tools for reappropriating the past are sharpened or blunted by the contemporary state of scientific and historical knowledge. We experience this phenomenon vividly today with the passing of the sacred languages of the Christian past from the knowledge and even the awareness of the great majority of Christians. Tradition changes as we receive it differently from the past and as we interpret it differently in the light of the future. In other words, there is no tradition without a development. Development of doctrine—to use a phrase which may not be entirely felicitous—is an integral part of the successiveness of tradition as hermeneutics of the Christian situation. If I use the term *hermeneutics* here—for the first time in this lecture—this is not because the term is in fashion. The fashion in question makes it so comprehensive that it has in fact lost all concrete meaning. I use it precisely because reading the past in the light of the future—which I call tradition—is always rereading, and there is no rereading without an interpretation of what we read. This was called hermeneutics before the meaning of this term was overextended into covering the entire process of knowledge.[13]

In the light of this analysis, one may venture a conclusion concerning the polemics of the sixteenth century about *scriptura sola:* in the main, the debates of the Reformation missed the real question. Nobody seems to have been aware of the true nature and structure of the tradition that was talked about, challenged by the ones and defended by the others with an equal misunderstanding of the matter. For the Catholic polemicists with few exceptions, tradition acted as a general storehouse of arguments to defend points that were denied or questioned by the Reformers. For the Reformers, tradition, as it had been handed down from the Middle Ages, was responsible for all the abuses that needed to be reformed; it therefore had to be attacked at its very basis as a man-made system which stifled the gospel. In both cases, tradition was simply the uncritical sum total of the church's past. This past naturally contained a good deal of errors and abuses, as well as many good and holy things. On one side of the sixteenth century crisis, one paid attention chiefly to the abuses, and tradition had to be rejected as a norm of faith. On the other side, most that one saw in the church's past seemed to be good and holy, and tradition was maintained as the permanent postapostolic norm of faith.[14]

In order to see the real problem of tradition, it would have been necessary to notice that each side had proceeded to its own selection and interpretation. This had been made according to opposite principles but according to the same structural process. In affirming the tradition in the bull *Regnans in excelsis,* by which he condemned Luther, Leo X did what Luther had himself done when he condemned the tradition in *The Babylonian Captivity of the Church.* Both selected from, and interpreted, the historical data with an insufficient critique of their principles of selection and of hermeneutics. At the Leipzig Disputation, Johannes Eck maintained the infallibility of general councils, which Luther denied. But neither one noticed that they reached contradictory conclusions by walking along one and the same path: each judged the past in the light of the present as he understood it. Neither one was able to notice what an adequate analysis of their methodology should have brought to light: the tradition they talked about, which the one accepted and the other rejected, did not exist in itself. Tradition comes to existence only *in nobis;* there is no *in se* here. Tradition lives as tradition in the hermeneutical proc-

ess by which a theologian, criticizing the testimonies of the
Christian past, assesses their value for the present and the
future. Such an evaluation can be negative or positive.
Whatever its sign, the process remains the same. In other
words, the real problem of tradition concerns two aspects.
First, how do we read the testimonies of the past, whether
these are theological, doctrinal, canonical, or liturgical?
Second, how do we reconstruct for the present and the
future a living synthesis of what the authors of the past
constructed for their time?

To this type of question, Catholics have commonly given
an answer which seems quite insufficient today. They have
tended to say that theologians must listen first of all to the
living *magisterium* and its more or less frequent instructions
concerning the shape of the tradition. They have argued or
simply assumed that, under the guidance of the Spirit, the
magisterium enjoys charisms of discernment by which it will
make the proper selection of documents from the past and
state its conclusions with trustworthy authority. Such a con-
fidence in the institutional guidance of the Spirit takes little
account of the fact that, confronted with the Christian past,
the members of the hierarchy are exactly in the same position as the theologians and the faithful. The bishop or the
pope who wishes to teach a point of faith or morals with
authority faces the same dilemma as the theologian who
seeks to clear up a point of the doctrinal or theological
tradition. Both must select and analyze the patrimony of the
church; they must reconstruct its datum and assess its value
for the present. Theologians of the Counter Reformation
and, still more, the manualists of the nineteenth and twen-
tieth centuries often abandoned the burden of spiritual
discernment to bishops. But the theologians' problem cannot be shouldered by the bishops, who should not be
blamed for the shortcomings and mistakes of theologians.
For the bishop stands to the past in the same relation as the

theologian. At the most he will feel an official responsibility which theologians may not experience in the same way and to the same extent. But, if it is to have persuasive value rather than be imposed and accepted on the basis of power, the methodology of the magisterium should be exactly that of theological reflection, namely, it should reflect on the past with a view to its reconstruction for today in the light of the anticipated future. Facing the past, people, theologians, bishops, popes, councils are in identical positions. In all cases, they have to reinterpret and reconstruct the witness of the past. And if, once reconstructed and coming alive, the tradition ever speaks effectively, this is always through the concrete medium of persons of flesh and blood.

IV

To the same type of question, Protestants have commonly given an answer which is no less unsatisfactory.

Both Lutheran and Calvinist orthodoxy, in the seventeenth and eighteenth centuries, paid great attention to the Latin Fathers and especially to Augustine. They did so on the ground that the Fathers followed the scriptures and were in agreement with these. This had been the attitude during the Sacramentarian controversy as it was the doctrine of the *Institutes* of Calvin. The principle did not change with the popularity of the appeal to tradition in Protestant orthodoxy. The basis for the Protestant argument *ex traditione* was the scripture, not the tradition as such. Yet no theologian could have concluded that the Fathers agreed with *scriptura sola,* unless he had himself interpreted and reconstructed both the thought of the Fathers and the witness of scripture. And this he could do only with the very same methodology by which Catholics interpreted and reconstructed the tradition. The difference between the two sides did not lie in their methods, but in that Protestants

restricted tradition to its early scriptural stages whereas
Catholics extended it to the entire postapostolic period.
The *scriptura sola* of the Reformers constituted an exclusive
norm of faith and theology once it had been judged to be
unique, and uniquely binding, by theologians sorting out
the past in the light of the present for the sake of the future.
The distinction between *scriptura sola* and *scriptura et traditio*
was, as it were, a distinction without a difference. It did not
bear on the essence and structure of the theological method, but on its application. The Reformers functioned with a
self-imposed restriction to *scriptura sola*, which was no less
interpreted and hermeneuticized at their hands for being
thought to be scripture-imposed and scripture-verified.

Once again, the problem does not reside where the sixteenth century, the Counter Reformation, and Protestant
orthodoxy placed it. Confronted with the past, Catholics
and Protestants are in an identical situation: in order to
know the past and to see it live, whether as scripture or as
tradition, they have to reconstruct it. The real problem of
tradition is methodological: according to what criteria can
historical documentation speak with a living voice, persuasive enough to become a norm of faith and behavior for
present generations?

V

At this point of my reflections, I will propose a paradoxi-
cal position: such criteria, in my opinion, do not exist. One
cannot formulate a universal method for the elaboration
and interpretation of tradition except along the broadest
possible lines. A theological method judged to be valid for
all times and all places can be a general structure, but not a
detailed model. The only concrete criterion which actually
functions is the consciousness of the theologian, of the
bishop, of the pope, and the corporate consciousness which

emerges through the debates of a council. The judgment by which one concludes that the voice of the tradition has spoken and is still valid or, on the contrary, has lost its relevance, is so closely tied to the personal experience of faith that one cannot find universal criteria for it. Such a judgment is composed of variables. The only elements that appear to be constant are the presence of Christ and the guidance of the Spirit, this presence and this guidance being manifested in an experience which is always unique and ultimately incommunicable. In the question of tradition, we therefore deal with a criterion which is also and at the same time a noncriterion. We face an absolute criterion, God in Christ and in the Spirit, whose awareness in us can only be relative.

There follow several consequences.

There is no essential difference between the Catholic trust in, and the Protestant distrust for, tradition. In both cases a selection has been made in the evidence left to us from the past. No one takes in without question what history tells him. Each one on the contrary chooses his texts according to a line of orthodoxy which he has himself drawn. He chooses his texts because he recognizes them as authentic witnesses of faith, but they are authentic witnesses insofar as he himself has established or accepted criteria of authenticity and orthodoxy. By and large, Protestants follow principles relating to the material order of the contents of faith. Thus, in the typical case of Martin Luther, the doctrine of justification by faith is the material principle in the light of which all Christianity is judged. Catholics prefer principles of the formal order: they are likely to assess the authority of a document or of a doctrine by reference to their origin. If this origin happens to be unknown, they fall back on the formal principle of the analogy of faith: is the doctrine or the document in question in harmony with the general lines of Catholic thought?

Yet the choice of a formal or of a material criterion of orthodoxy and of tradition does not constitute an essential difference. In some cases, a formal criterion is alone applicable. Thus, if the meaning of a doctrine is no longer apparent (as, for instance, in the case of the belief in virginity *in partu*), its value can still emerge from an investigation of its origin, if such an investigation can be made satisfactorily. Furthermore, the *magisterium* of the Catholic church itself uses a formal or a material criterion according to diverse contexts. For instance, the legitimate authority of the Council of Chalcedon is recognized in keeping with its ecumenicity (formal criterion), but that of its twenty-eighth canon is commonly rejected on account of its content (material criterion). A similar remark can be made about the fifth session of the Council of Constance. Thus, even for Catholics at the highest levels of authority, the form is not always a sure warrant for orthodoxy. The full Catholic criterion for the Catholic tradition would be the concordance of a formal criterion (the source or organ which teaches a doctrine) and a material criterion (the agreement of a doctrine with the sum total of the other Catholic doctrines). This material criterion is itself dependent on the formal principal of the analogy of faith. But if this is a correct picture of the facts, one must simply renounce the hope that we may have at our disposal absolute criteria that may serve as touch-stones of orthodoxy. Here again, the enlightened awareness of the theologian needs to act as catalyst.

Whence a second conclusion: freedom of debate and the allowance of a variety of opinions are indispensable for the tradition eventually to emerge from the past. Only from a comparison of divergent opinions can light be obtained on their relative value. Accordingly, freedom of expression in the church is not a luxury, but a requirement of the intelligibility of faith. The time needed for a serene discussion of divergences in matters of faith will allow the Spirit to manifest himself without hindrance and to create step by step the unanimity of believers.

Thirdly, the Spirit alone is, in final analysis, the absolute criterion of the Christian faith, and therefore of tradition, and therefore of the emergence of tradition through the interpretation of the past by theologians or by the *magisterium* of the churches. And the only criterion of this faith and of this tradition which is at the same time practical, proximate, and ascertainable is the moral unanimity of the disciples: by this we know that the Spirit has shown himself. This entails no negative conclusion concerning the magisterium and its intrinsic authority. It requires, however, that the *magisterium* be set in the context of the catholicity, the unanimity, the collegiality, the conciliarity, the sobornost, of the church and the manifestation of this *consensus in the sensus fidelium*.

Fourthly, a remarkable convergence may then be seen among three points of view. Eastern orthodoxy has always stressed unanimity as a condition of true tradition; since the Counter Reformation, Catholicism has emphasized the structural authority of diverse organs in the institution of the church; classical Protestantism, both Lutheran and Calvinist, found the effective criteria of doctrine in the content of biblical faith in relation to the core doctrines of redemption and justification. Yet in all three cases, the decision as to what tradition is emerges always in the living consciousness of believers. It is the faithful—pope, bishop, priest, deacon, laity—who are able to judge for themselves the value of the criterion selected and the mode of its application. Divergences do no more than cover up a remarkable methodological convergence. But if such is the case, the problem of tradition amounts to the question of discerning the Spirit. All Christian believers and communities need to sharpen their spiritual sensitivity. Tradition emerges when the faithful interpret the memory of the past as normative for the faith of the future. But this can be done only through the discernment of the Spirit after a sustained and graceful *metanoia*.

Notes

1. *On the school of T*übingen, cf. Josef Geiselmann, *Die lebendige Überlieferung als Norm des Christlichen Glauben* (Freiburg-im-Breisgau, 1958); on the school of Rome, cf. J. P. Mackey, *The Modern Theology of Tradition* (London, 1962).

2. Yves Congar, *La Tradition et les Traditions* (Paris, 1960) pp. 239–42.

3. Heiko Oberman, "Quo Vadis, Petre? The History of Tradition from Irenaeus to *Humani Generis*," *Harvard Divinity School Bulletin* (1962) pp. 1–25.

4. George Tavard, *La Tradition au XVIIe siècle* (Paris, 1970) pp. 55–78.

5. Cf. *Le Mystère du Surnaturel* (Paris, 1965); *Augustinisme et Théologie Moderne* (Paris, 1965).

6. *Holy Writ or Holy Church* (New York, 1959); *The Quest for Catholicity* (New York, 1963); *Woman in Christian Tradition* (Notre Dame, 1973).

7. *La Tradition au XVIIe siècle*, p. 486.

8. Fernand Guimet, *Existence et Eternité* (Paris, 1973).

9. *La Tradition au XVIIe siècle*, p. 486.

10. *L'Action* (Paris, 1893); *L'Action*, 2 vols. (Paris, 1936–37).

11. Especially with Saint John of the Cross (*The Ascent of Mount Carmel*).

12. On the connection between mission and the development of doctrine, see my recent volume, *La Théologie parmi les Sciences Humaines* (Paris, 1975).

13. See my remarks on hermeneutics in the next lecture.

14. *Holy Writ or Holy Church.*

CHAPTER SIX

Tradition In Theology: A
Methodological Approach

George H. Tavard

So far I have studied the problem of tradition as it emerges in the light of the controversies between Protestants and Catholics, especially at the time of the Reformation. These reflections should now be completed in a more systematic way in relation to contemporary theological methodology. By this I hope to be able to carry the problem further and perhaps to envision a suitable solution. I will begin with some thoughts on the requirements of a theological method. For it seems to me that methodology, as applied to theological work, should make a positive contribution to the question of tradition. Methodology is also a fashionable topic for discussion. This may be accidental to our treatment of the matter; yet it indicates a need which ought not be ignored.

I

Among older authors—such as the scholastics, who are unjustly disdained by some of the new theologies of our day—theological reflection was itself the object of theological reflection. The *Summa theologica* of Thomas Aquinas even takes it as the first topic of reflection, at least in the presentation of the *Summa* if not in the chronology of its conception and perhaps not in the order of thought. At any rate, in the form in which medieval theology has reached us, if not in that of its actual teaching and of its oral discussion in the Schools, a primary place is given to the question of method, as treated in many prologues to Commentaries on the Sentences and to *Summae*.

Reflection on theological method is not only methodology, as Bernard Lonergan suggests in his book, *Method in Theology*. It is itself theology. And I would like to call it *general* theology, to distinguish it both from *particular* theologies (the theological systems of the various authors) and from special theologies (the monographic tractates on God, the Trinity, the Creation, etc.). Each author has his own particular system, even though he may not have attempted to develop it fully, still less to write it. Each theological statement contains in itself the proportions of a complete system, just as a section of a jawbone discovered in a paleontological stratum contains the proportions of the entire skeleton to which it belongs.

By and large, contemporary authors favor less formally structured essays than was the case formerly. I would regard these as corresponding to a *synthetic* type of theology, differing from the analytic type in which the schoolmen excelled. I see no reason to abandon the expression, *positive* or *historical* theology (not positivistic or, despite Gordon Kaufmann, historicist theology), to designate the studies where hypothesis and thesis are chiefly tested by a historical investigation of the past. Likewise, *systematic, philosophical,* or *speculative* theology may be retained for the studies where history and scriptural exegesis remain auxiliary to the hypothesis and the thesis; I prefer "systematic," however, as being more indicative of what is important in a theological synthesis, namely its coherence.

In other words, theology is many-faceted. And yet I believe—and this will be my thesis in the following pages—that all these aspects of the theological work would be not only historically impossible but also theoretically inconceivable if they were not organized around a preexisting kernel, or, to change the metaphor, strung along a previously woven thread. This kernel or thread I identify with the tradition, or at least with a tradition. The difference between *the* and *a* in this context will be made clearer later on.

Facing the wide conspectus of these various types of theology—to which one could add the qualified theologies that have been in the news recently, such as black theology, political theology, and also, though more hypothetically, all conceivable theologies that no one has yet thought of—general theology remarks that each type of theology is historically and logically prepared by a *pretheology* which makes its emergence historically possible and logically consistent. Just as there is no physics without a mathematics which is antecedent to it, there is no theology without a ground which nurtures the rise of a new system. Whether this system reaches more than embryonic or fragmentary form remains relatively unimportant. In the evolution of theological methodology, ways of studying, listening, reading, of analyzing, criticizing, judging, have appeared at one time or another, in one place or another, precisely in relation to certain ways of thought that are broader than each theology and that allow all theologies to find their proper shape.

Relevance, about which we are excessively concerned today, corresponds to the surface texture of thought; depth of thought is related to the memory of a past and to the anticipation of a future. Each theological system adds a link to a given tradition without which it would remain an unthinkable ephapax. If theo-logy, in its etymological sense, implies "knowledge of God," it requires both thought and language. Or, in keeping with the acknowledgement that no thought subsists without language, theology implies the language that enables man to think about God. Language is synchronic: it does express a semantic and a syntactic system according to which sounds are used in a certain way, familiar to a given historical collectivity. But language is also diachronic: the language we speak is the product of a long evolution of manners of speech. The language of our day results from that of the day before as modified by those who actually speak it. But theologies are languages, since they are discourses. Their structure, as present discourses about God, presuppose past ways of discoursing about God. (I use the word *discourse* to denote a limited sum of theological insights as they relate to each other in their formulation.) The past ways thus presupposed by a theology form the tradition in which the theology in question is necessarily inserted.

It would be absurd to believe that some theologies—say, scholasticism, or the theology of the Reformers—appeared in their time by the operation of the Holy Spirit without being in most ways the product of an accountable evolution from the past. Each theological system makes sense when it is seen in the context of its tradition. However prophetic it may be claimed to be by its followers, however advanced it may be considered by its surprised or enthusiastic contemporaries, however new it may have seemed at one time, it was itself a crossroads where a wealth of spiritual experiences and intellectual movements which preceded and prepared it converged.

Indeed, one should be able to detect three levels in all theological discourse. There is a level of supraconsciousness: the insights encapsulated in a discourse are related in some way to the superconsciousness of God's self-revelation, which is usually called faith. There is a level of consciousness: the discourse formulates insights of which the theologian is clearly aware in his own self-knowledge. All theological discourse also unveils a preconscious level, consisting of structural underpinnnings inherited from the past, inherent in the ways of thinking adopted, and without which the other two levels would not see the light of formulation. It is precisely at this level that one discovers the locus of the tradition which underlies a theological system.

By their very nature, the supraconscious and the preconscious may escape attention until methodological reflection brings them to light. The supraconscious inspires symbols; because it lies beyond consciousness by excess of light it tends to find expresson indirectly in the symbolism of theological systems. The preconscious remains, of itself, beneath consciousness because awareness of it requires a certain distanciation between oneself as subject and oneself as object. Yet both precede the conscious level in the total theological experience; and the conscious level is fed by them.

II

The tradition is not only a pretheology. It is also a *posttheology*. For tradition is never finished and it remains always in the making. An aspect of tradition may be perceived when critical examination unveils the epistemological assumptions and the noetic structures of a theological system. This can fully appear only after the discourse has been made and studied. As pretheology, chronologically anterior to theology, tradition acts as a precomprehension in relation to this posttheology, as an anticipation in which the up-building of a future theological system is already outlined. This is to say that tradition passes through a propedeutic stage. As such it is past; we have inherited it; we retain it in the form of memory. From there it enters a critical stage (in the sense of the exercise of the critical faculty, not in the sense that a crisis is created). This critical stage is best approached through the objective critique of our own discourse by others. Self-critique is undoubtedly possible. Yet is is always difficult to treat our own system, our personal synthesis, as objects to be evaluated with detachment in a spirit of scientific criticism.

One may note at this point that, in theological criticism as elsewhere, science never amounts to a collection of individual facts. A knowledge may be called scientific when, prompted by the facts as we know them, we proceed to make hypotheses regarding, if not an exhaustive universality of facts, at least a generality that may be verified in relation to many facts. In this sense there is no science of the singular, but always of the universal. And yet a theological system is always individual and particular. The critique of theological knowledge has therefore the primary task of eliciting from the particularity of its object the universal or general elements that are comprehensible to all who enjoy a precomprehension of it, recognizable to all who have mastered enough of the elements of its recognition, acceptable by all who share the premises of the theology under study.[1]

But that which is shared, that which, in the light of faith and under the guidance of rationality and historicality, emerges as being potentially universal in the particularity of a theological discourse, gains its universality from being related to the universal structures of thought and of theology. Within particular, special, synthetic, analytic, positive, systematic theologies there lies a core, a structure of spiritual experience and of intellectual achievement, which I identify with tradition. By hypothesis, the universal must be both antecedent and subsequent to the particular since, if it is universal it is to be found already in the theological systems of past ages, and it will be found still in the systems of ages yet to come. Thus the pretheology which is tradition is in necessary continuity with the posttheology of all theological systems. When a discourse has been examined, when a system has been more or less completed and studied, tradition is seen both as the past from which the discourse has derived and as the future toward which it is propedeutically oriented.

Yet when a theologian explains his method to assist his readers, when, with honesty and objectivity, he unfolds the pretheology out of which he comes and which runs like an undercurrent in all his discourse, he does not thereby reveal the eschatological tension of his thought toward the future developments that are implicit in his system. Between its past as pretheology and its future as posttheology, tradition cannot but evolve. It evolves at least insofar as this particular theology contributes to its development. The postface says more than the preface; the epilogue adds something to the prologue. Admittedly, there must always be a recognizable link of continuity from the one to the other. Yet what a theologian has effectively done is not always what he intended to do. Insofar as he was aware of his tradition or pretheology, he may have elaborated a theoretical method. Yet it is only from the effective emergence of his tradition as posttheology that one may gauge his real method. The distinction between theoretical method and real method is closely related to the difference between pretheology and posttheology, between the tradition from the past and the tradition into the future.

This distinction may be illustrated fairly easily. A typical case seems to be that of Paul Tillich, a theologian who was more concerned with method than most of his colleagues. At the beginning of his *Systematic Theology*, Tillich announces that he will use a method of correlation: phenomenological analysis of the human situation will ask a question to which theological analysis of the revelation in the Christ will provide an answer. Revelation responds to existential philosophy. Accordingly, the main hinges of Tillich's system will turn around correlations between being and God, existence and the Christ, life and the Spirit, history and the church.

But does Tillich always follow this clearly described method? If he was only a philosopher searching for transcendental responses to existential questions, he might find such responses in the Christian revelation. But Tillich was also a Christian in search of philosophical correlations for his faith. He was obviously aware of the answer before formulating the question. Whence the critical suspicion that the question was predetermined by the answer. Tillich would have admitted indeed that the form of the question depends on the form of the answer. (In Thomism, also, the ultimate determination of matter derives from the form.) But one should go further: Is not the substance of the question itself dependent upon the substance of the answer which Tillich intends to provide? Should the existential question be asked by a Zen Buddhist, the Christian answer would constitute no response, as Tillich seems to have realized in the journey to Japan which he made in the last years of his career. For neither question nor answer would be tailored to each other: the question would be formulated so independently of the answer that it could not be answered. There is no answer to a *koan*. In such a case, then, the theoretical correlation between question and answer cannot be identified with the real correlation. In the theoretical correlation, asking the question of existence includes a precomprehension of the answer which will allow the answer to be understood and accepted. In the real correlation, it is the answer which permits the question of existence to be asked in such a way that it will be answered. Just as redemption, in the Pauline letters, reveals the logically previous fall, the revelation elicits the logically previous existential question. Thus the movement of thought which Tillich's pretheology projects is the reverse of the movement of thought which a critical analysis discovers.

The connection of this with the problem of tradition should be clear. The tradition which a critical student sees at work in a discourse or in a finished system has grown past the stage of the same tradition at which the system began to take shape or the discourse to be composed. The posttheology is not identical with the pretheology. A projected method represents the stage of a tradition at which an author considers himself to be, and it suggests how he hopes to carry this tradition further. The achieved method represents the stage of the tradition at which the theologian comes out, and it shows what he has actually done to carry the tradition further.

The source of this difference within a continuous tradition is not far to seek. At the stage of pretheology, in which the tradition is received as an inherited patrimony pregnant with many possibilities, the theological discourse does not yet exist. It may be foreseen in the form of a desire or of a dream, but it has yet no more consistence than a dream. If we may speak here of reasoning reason and thinking thought (according to the vocabulary of Maurice Blondel), reasoned reason, thought thought, formulated conception, acted action are not yet. Theology is not yet discourse, not yet *logos*. It is still silence. From there to the moment when it has been reasoned, thought, formulated, acted, one has to cross an abyss that can be spanned only by the activity of building the theological system. And action, the passage from potency to act, always brings about alterations in the projected mode of action. As we know well enough from the works of Karl Marx, action always transforms the project to which it is applied. The difference between tradition as pretheology and tradition as posttheology is commensurate with the creative power of the theological activity involved in a given project. Once a theologian has described the method he plans to use and which he sees, in his propedeutic vision, as consistent with the tradition he has inherited and accepted, he still remains open to modification of the project that he has envisaged by the subject that he is. Here, as elsewhere, thought is shaped by praxis. The tradition before and the tradition after the action differ with the exact scope of the praxis.

III

In my understanding, one cannot make a sharp distinction between the tradition and the traditions. Such a difference in vocabulary has become familiar to many. It is embodied in the Faith and Order report on "Scripture, Tradition and the Traditions" (Montreal). It provides the title of Yves Congar's book on the subject. Although it does not appear in the constitution *Dei Verbum* of Vatican II, it dominates a recent speech of Pope Paul VI, from which I will quote these lines:

> We ought to explain here what we understand by tradition in the religious sense. With the Holy Scriptures it constitutes the revelation and, with the assistance of the Holy Spirit and through the magisterium, it transmits the revelation in a way which is authentic and binding.... And this tradition should be distinguished from what is usually called traditions, which are rather habits, customs, styles, transitory and changing forms of human life, devoid of the charism of a truth which would make them immutable and binding. We will even add that these purely historical and human traditions not only contain many contingent and imperfect elements which criticism may freely judge and reform, but also must often be criticized and reformed because of the ease with which human things grow old, get twisted and need to be purified and replaced.[2]

What is called here the tradition is made up of a number of distinct and not always mutually consistent traditions.

These are modes of thinking and feeling, of life and action (thought and feeling are themselves forms of life and action) which have been sufficiently embodied in lasting works (writings, paintings, sculptures, liturgies, ways of prayers, linguistic habits) to influence later generations. Such traditions are in constant mutation. There is not only a flow, but also a flux, of the traditions. In what sense we may still speak of the tradition we shall see further on. The point I wish to emphasize at this time is precisely that the involvement of all Christian experience in a stage before and a stage after renders tradition necessarily fluent. Each theologian contributes to this flux. Having elaborated a project, devised a method, caught a glimpse of a goal, he discovers little by little that the projected form has changed through the impact of his own action upon it, that the method has shifted ground, that the attained goal no longer looks as the preliminary glimpse of it from a distance had led him to expect.

But if this is so, if a necessary dichotomy separates potency and act, project and realization, pretheology and posttheology, the ante- and post-phases of tradition, we are entitled to expect theologians to show awareness of the phenomenon of drift to which they are subject in the course of their work. Ultimately they will presumably select their final position, if they ever reach a final position, as being the real, the authentic one. Yet such a final position will be fully understandable and will make the best sense only in the light of the drift which preceded it in methodology, in the accumulation and interpretation of documents, in the tentative adoption and discarding of models, in the checking and counter-checking of verification, in the succession of diverse foci, in the identification and the organization of the theological horizon.[3]

In other words, tradition is not only a pretheology and a posttheology in relation to a theological discourse or system. It is also what I will call, with some danger of misunderstanding, an *infratheology*. The evolution of tradition under the impact of its use in theological elaboration should not be so hidden within the theologian's undercurrents of thought that it does not reach consciousness. I do not employ the term infratheology in analogy with the subconscious or the unconscious. As infratheology, tradition underlies all theological work, but it can be easily reached by reflexive attention. Whether the theological effort aims at hypothesis, at synthesis, at historical interpretation or at systematic speculation, theologians should constantly check their conceived and apparent method with the transformation, deformation, reformation which theological praxis imprints upon it, shaping their real method, changing their pretheology into their posttheology, imposing a certain curve upon the tradition within which they work with the inevitable consequence that they also work upon it.

I do not wish the expression infratheology to imply derogatory connotations. Perhaps one could speak here of a supratheology, but the danger of triumphalism is always greater with intellectuals than that of humiliationism. One could suggest intratheology; this would have the advantage of hinting at the interiority of tradition, which lives within the heart of all theological work. Or *sub*theology, but this might suggest subconsciousness as its normal state, a suggestion which I would find unfortunate. No doubt, *meta*theology would appeal both to those who still think of metaphysics and to those who already think, with modern researchers in these domains, of metamathematics or metalanguage. Yet I would find it ambiguous, since I have already reserved the etymologically bastard yet literally identical expression of posttheology in another sense.

To describe tradition as an infratheology means that tradition is not only, in relation to a theology, past and future. It is also present. It underlies every theological movement and it is transformed by such a movement.

There is no theological praxis without tradition working within it. But then, given the wide spectrum of Christian theologies, one may well wonder about the consistency of tradition: is there one tradition? Are there many? Is there a unity within the multiplicity of traditions that are available to theologians and that have so been used that theological systems have contradicted one another? This is the question of the tradition and the traditions.

IV

What is *the* tradition? In the address I have quoted, Pope Paul starts from a theological concept of the tradition as the Spirit-guided transmission of the deposit of the Christian faith. To such a tradition one can only take on, as subordinate, unavoidable in their generality but always expendable in their particularity, the many traditions that have had their day in the complex life and thought of the people of God. I would rather reverse the perspective and start from these imperfect, constantly reformable, yet ever present traditions. Each theologian is faced with a multiple choice. What will he select, in the immense wealth of the Christian past, as the signposts of his own research? I envisage *the* tradition as the sum total of all that has so far been accumulated in Christian experience and is therefore available for information and documentation, for interpretation and hermeneutics, for the selection of a theological focus and its setting in a horizon of thought and life, for the building of theological models and for their verification. Taken in this sense, the tradition is normative; for there is no other source of past insights and no other recourse for checks and balances according to the experience of the past. But it is perceived in its capacity as norm of thought and life only to the extent that each person has discovered and adopted a principle for seeking among the many monuments of the past and for sifting out what has become too old to be used and what remains new enough to be put in the new urns of prospective theological research. At this point, the old polemics between Catholics and Protestants about "free interpretation" have become pointless. Whenever one adopts a principle of selection or chooses a principle of interpretation, one does exercise "free interpretation" as a duty and therefore as a right. In his address about tradition, Paul VI warns against the danger of

> claiming to give the Christian faith a personal, original, arbitrary interpretation; this is the "free interpretation" (*libero esame*) which takes no account of the teaching of those who have the duty of "keeping the deposit."[4]

This is of course an echo of past misunderstandings and polemics; it shows that the misunderstandings are not entirely past, and one suspects that this is so on all sides. The reality of the tradition is more complex than this passage would suggest. In any case, understanding of the past is necessarily personal; it can, if our insights are creative enough, be also original; it need never be, if we are well-informed and responsible, arbitrary.

What is the role of the tradition? In my understanding of the theological task, each theologian chooses his intellectual and spiritual, even his confessional, tradition from the multiplicity of the many Christian traditions, the sum total of which may be called the tradition. He makes his choice none the less for simply inheriting the past into which he has been born and educated. To refuse to choose some other tradition, to abstain from studying other traditions sufficiently to be able to make an informed choice among them: these are also the outcome of a decision, namely, the decision to follow the tradition into which one has been born and educated. In relation to each theological discourse, the tradition constitutes a universal horizon which can provide us, if we wish, with points of comparison, signposts, points of view, that will enable us to criticize our own work. Within this tradition we find all our tools and we learn to use them. Thus tradition presents itself to us as a repertory of signs, as a language to decipher, as a universe of symbols. We bring to it principles of organization and of interpretation. But we can bring these principles to bear upon these signs because we have seen how the universe of symbols was organized and interpreted in the past. Theology is always a hermeneutics of what is contained in the tradition as the universal horizon of the Christian community. In relation to theology, therefore, the tradition is the permanent reservoir of pieces for construction and reconstruction, and of points of reference for the critique that must be made of theology as of all creations of the human mind.

In relation to the Church and its faith, the tradition has a similar function. It is the memory of the community, identical with the entirety of the Christian past in as far as the past has left visible traces. The whole community should not only transmit its patrimony, its tradition; it should also return to it periodically for self-criticism and self-reform. Pope Paul rightly remarks:

> The tradition, the true tradition, is a root, not a chain; it is an irreplaceable patrimony, a wealth, a vital fidelity. It is not easy to state briefly in what this treasure consists, where the wise Christian draws old things and new things.[5]

Hermeneutics is a difficult task, which indeed requires a special charism. But this is the charism of the theological community, in which the charisms of each check against the charisms of all. I am not too sure that it is correct to say, as Pope Paul does, that this "special charism" is

> the charism of the church's *magisterium* which is certain of the assistance of the Spirit of truth, especially in decisive moments.[6]

There is of course a charism of authority. But to discern meanings, to translate symbols, to demythologize the past and to remythologize it in new ways, to read the languages of the past and to reformulate them in the languages of today and in those of tomorrow that are taking shape, is a complex process which requires much more than a charism of authority. Discernment is not achieved without trial and error, without mutual discussion and fraternal correction, without free and extensive exchange and critique. It is only in the total freedom of intellectual debate that *it* of the past can become the *I* of the present, if I may adopt a pregnant sentence of Freud: *Wo "es" war, soll "ich" werden*[7] (Where there was "it," there should be "I").

Thus, tradition may best be seen as a historical catena of all Christian symbols, as these are related to one another in the analogy of faith, and to all other human symbols in the analogy of creation (or, if we prefer, in the analogy of being). Theology is the art of reading and translating these symbols so that they yield meaning for the present and they help to prepare for and to anticipate the future. Such symbols are multiform. There are the symbols of the universe as God's creation; the symbols of human life and though as man's impact upon God's creation; the symbols of the Christian faith in its orthodox and its heterodox forms; faith itself as symbol of higher realities that "eyes have not seen and ears have not heard" (1 Cor. 2:9); the symbols created by all previous attempts at exegesis and hermeneutics. They yield meaning little by little in the practice of Christian life, so that, for from being a purely intellectual affair, theology requires a praxis of the faith, an intimate familiarity with the two poles of the Christian life, the scriptures and the sacraments.

This commitment, this engagement, and this praxis belong to the texture of theological activity and they point up the primacy of tradition as infratheology over tradition as pretheology and as posttheology. Similar in this to all other researchers, the theologian ought to know what he does. To be aware of his infratheology is not an expendable luxury reserved to introspective temperaments. It is a requirement of theology as spiritual activity. For if one can understand that all are not completely aware of their intellectual thought, if a relative ignorance of the structures of our *episteme* is forgivable, at least spiritual experience should normally lead us to discern the theological virtues at work in our life and therefore also in our theology as life and reflection.

Tradition as pretheology is memory sifted and restructured by imagination. Tradition as posttheology results from a critical examination which discerns the pattern of hope emerging from our reflection. Tradition as infratheology corresponds to the authentic living of the theological virtues or, in a less scholastic vocabulary, to the impact of the analogy of faith upon the structures of our noetic experience. In the very act of thinking, faith enlightens the inner processes of the intellect, changing our foreseen logic into a logic lived according to the demands of faith. In other words, infratheology requires, not only total intellectual authenticity, but also religious, mystical consciousness within the praxis of thinking. Theological elaboration should be transcendental by virtue of its inner dynamics, not only on account of the transcendence of its object. It feeds upon attention, not indeed the passing, peripheral attention sufficient for everyday life, but a deep and total attention, which may be identified with a full adherence of the will to God's dwelling and action in us, and to the corresponding sublimation of our intellectual faculties.

It is indeed difficult to observe ourself objectively at the moment when we, as subject, focus our attention on the divine object of theological science. Yet by the nature of this science the structure of theology is never entirely preordained; it emerges progressively as we do theology. Tradition as pretheology takes the shape of hypotheses that guide us. Tradition as infratheology controls the operations of our thinking so that our hypotheses are transformed into theses, whose spiritual coherence is no less important than their intellectual logic. Thus tradition underlies all theological processes as a basic attention which follows all the curves, faces all the difficulties, welcomes all the successes of the noetic enterprise of theology. It is an eye within the eye of faith.

Tradition as infratheology thus constitutes the proper link between pretheology and posttheology. Pretheology is anticipation and project; posttheology is eschatological orientation in the conclusions reached; infratheology is interior to the act of theologizing, to the thought that is in the process of being thought.

V

This raises the problem called, since John Henry Newman, the development of doctrine. If tradition is indeed, as I have tried to show, the stuff out of which all theologies are made because it is itself made of all theologies, then it must also be the element, not only of continuity between the past and the future of the theological enterprise, but also of growth from the past to the future.

In his address of August 7, 1974, Paul VI touched on this question:

The doctrine of faith is not without a logical and coherent development, which willingly responds to the needs of thought and to the duties of contemplation, according to St. Paul's exhortation to "grow in the knowledge of God" (Col. 1:17). But it remains univocal and faithful to its essential and original sense, equal to itself, such as Christ announced it and such as, today still, for the salvation of men and with the help of the Holy Spirit, the church proclaims it, defends it and orients it toward the infinite vision of the ineffable divine reality.[8]

Yet, despite Pope Paul's view, one thing is clear about tradition as the sum total of all Christian symbols: it is not univocal. Univocity would imply so complete a redundancy in the successive stages of tradition that one could not even speak of fidelity to itself: fidelity to itself requires distanciation from itself, and therefore nonredundancy, and therefore nonunivocity. A univocal tradition can only be apprehended in an unmoving fundamentalist attitude. And it matters little if this is the scripture-fundamentalism of Protestants or the church-fundamentalism of Catholics. In both cases the tradition has been mummified and is no longer alive. A tradition that comes to light age after age in several natural languages, in a succession of scriptures, creeds, councils, liturgies, implies linguistic polyvalence. The meanings of the expressions of the tradition, as they are historically, intentionally, and theologically related to one another, may be analogical. But the analogy in question is nearer to equivocity than to univocity. The languages used do not cease to be diverse for attempting to formulate the fidelity of many generations to a common substance of faith. Such a diversity is manifold. For tradition is couched not only in several natural languages (the number of which is multiplied as the tradition is geographically and culturally enlarged by the missionary witness) but also in many technical languages. Each council forges a new language to meet the needs of the times. Each theology creates its own language, as I have tried to show in my recent volume, *La Théologie parmi les Sciences Humaines.* Thus, tradition, taken as a whole, is polylinguistic; it cannot possibly be univocal.

Admittedly, Paul VI's concern is legitimate: How can we safeguard the continuity of tradition within the many processes of its development? Such a continuity is not protected by univocity. But it is guaranteed by the concept of tradition as the sum total of Christian symbols that fill the horizon of faith and come to life in the succession of theological hermeneutics. Yet there is no guarantee of logical growth and no evidence that the general coherence of the process will always be perceived. The church cannot escape the burden of constantly reforming itself.

* * *

Thus, the methodological approach adopted in this lecture ends up at the same point as the problematic, historical approach of my previous lecture. *Metanoia, catharsis,* self-reform, are works of the Spirit in the hearts of the faithful. The church in our times is called to closer listening to the Spirit. It finds itself confronting dilemmas for which it does not feel prepared. The end of the second milennium after Christ is bringing about a major crisis of civilization. Where can the Christian community discover the wisdom and the strength to weather the storm and to guide those of mankind who are looking for a Christian message in our times? We may look for wisdom and strength in the gospel, in the scriptures, in the tradition as the accumulated wisdom of the past. Yet only through purity of heart will wisdom emerge from the documents explaining the gospel, from the scriptures, from the monuments and texts of the past. At the present juncture, both history and theory call us to conversion.

Notes

1. Concerning these methodological principles, I may refer to *La Théologie parmi les Sciences Humaines* (Paris, 1975).
2. "Address at the general audience" of August 7, 1974 (Italian text: *L'Osservatore Romano,* August 8, 1974).

3. See *La Théologie parmi les Sciences Humaines.*
4. See note 2.
5. See note 2.
6. See note 2.
7. This sentence concludes *The Psychopathology of Everyday Life.* One will be aware of its importance in Jacques Lacan's interpretation of Freud.
8. See note 2.

Index